MOD PODGE ROCKS!

DECOUPAGE YOUR WORLD

Amy Anderson

LARKCRAFTS

Asheville

LARK CRAFTS

An Imprint of Sterling Publishing
387 Park Avenue South
New York, NY 10016

If you have questions or comments about
this book, please visit: larkcrafts.com

Editor: Linda Kopp
Art Director: Kristi Pfeffer
Photographer: Steve Carrell
Cover Designer: Kristi Pfeffer
Editorial Assistance:
Dawn Dillingham, Ginny Roper

MOD PODGE® is a registered
trademark of Plaid Enterprises, Inc.,
Norcross, Georgia, USA.
All rights reserved.

ISBN 978-1-4547-0241-2

Library of Congress Cataloging-in-Publication Data

Anderson, Amy (Amy Lauren), 1977-
 Mod podge rocks! : decoupage your world / Amy Anderson.
   p. cm.
 Includes index.
 ISBN 978-1-4547-0241-2 (pb-trade pbk. : alk. paper)
 1. Decoupage. I. Title.
 TT870.A4755 2012
 745.54'6--dc23

                                                    2011036218

Distributed in Canada by Sterling Publishing
c/o Canadian Manda Group, 165 Dufferin Street
Toronto, Ontario, Canada M6K 3H6
Distributed in the United Kingdom by GMC Distribution Services
Castle Place, 166 High Street, Lewes, East Sussex, England BN7 1XU
Distributed in Australia by Capricorn Link (Australia) Pty. Ltd.
P.O. Box 704, Windsor, NSW 2756, Australia

For information about custom editions, special sales, and premium and
corporate purchases, please contact Sterling Special Sales at 800-805-5489
or specialsales@sterlingpublishing.com.

Email academic@larkbooks.com for information about desk and examination copies.
The complete policy can be found at larkcrafts.com.

Every effort has been made to ensure that all the information in this book
is accurate. However, due to differing conditions, tools, and individual skills,
the publisher cannot be responsible for any injuries, losses, and other
damages that may result from the use of the information in this book.

Manufactured in China

6 8 10 9 7 5

larkcrafts.com

PROJECTS

Dear Readers,

I believe anyone can be creative. But I also believe each person needs to find what specifically works for him or her. I've been crafting since I was young, and have worked with a variety of materials, including yarn, fabric, and paint. It wasn't until I held up my first bottle of Mod Podge that I realized I had found the Holy Grail of crafting. Mod Podge is one of the few craft mediums that most people can pick up and use with little training—and get great results the very first time. It's hard to explain exactly what it is (beyond the fact that it's a glue, sealer, and finish) because nothing does Mod Podge justice more than using it. You'll see!

When I started my blog *Mod Podge Rocks* (www.modpodgerocksblog.com) in 2008, I never guessed that I would find hundreds of different project ideas that I liked and wanted to share with others. Not only is Mod Podge used for crafting, it is literally the glue that binds an entire community together. I have met some of the most amazing and talented people I have ever known through crafting and blogging. If you are not yet a member, I hope you will join us.

Whether you're a beginner or a novice, I believe you'll appreciate *Mod Podge Rocks!* This book includes a Mod Podge formula guide—which is my perspective on the various Mod Podge products and their best uses—basic instructions, and tons of projects and inspiration from me and some of my favorite Podgers. You'll find a wide variety of crafts ranging from home décor, gifts, kids' items, holiday projects, jewelry, and more. I'm happy to have many talented guest crafters in

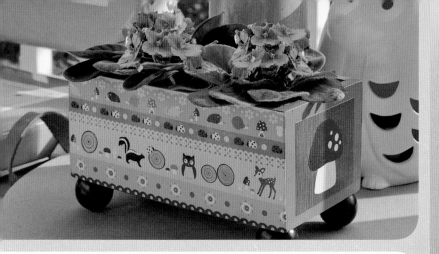

this book along with me, because you'll see Mod Podging from more than one perspective. I like to bring my personal favorites, bold colors, polka dots, and whimsy into what I do, so it's nice to see others share a bit of themselves as well.

The best way to learn to Mod Podge is to read through the basic instructions at the beginning of this book and then simply dive in to a project. Mod Podge is very forgiving, and if you have questions, I'm here for you. I hope you will enjoy Mod Podge as much as I do. Happy Podging!

All my best,

Amy Anna

Amy

P.S.
Here are some additional resources you might enjoy:
Mod Podge Rocks Facebook Fan Page – http://www.facebook.com/modpodgerocks
YouTube Instructional Videos: http://www.youtube.com/modpodgerocks
Plaid Enterprises - http://www.plaidonline.com/ModPodge

Primer

Here you go! *This section contains everything you need to know to make the great projects in this book. If you're a veteran Podger, you may want to review the information to remind yourself just how easy and simple Mod Podge® is to use. And, if you haven't worked with some of the other formulas, who knows, you may be inspired to try something new. For beginners, a few easy steps will lead you through the basic techniques, which will allow you to dive in to any project with guaranteed success. Ready?*

What Is Mod Podge?

Only the greatest decoupage medium on the face of the earth! Made in the U.S.A. by Plaid Enterprises, Inc., for over 45 years, crafters have used Mod Podge for their most treasured creations. This amazing all-in-one glue, sealer, and finish has come a long way since its invention in the 1960s. It's become a true favorite among crafters at all levels for its versatility, dependability, and value.

Just what can it do? It's glue that holds tight and dries clear for adhering paper, fabric, and other porous materials to almost any surface. It's a sealer that protects decoupage, acrylic paint, stain, fabric, and more. And it's a finish that's durable, smooth, and fast-drying. Because it's non-toxic with simple soap and water cleanup, Mod Podge is perfect when crafting with kids. Plus, it now comes in a variety of formulas and finishes suited for specific uses.

What's the Difference Between Mod Podge Formulas?

This is one of the most frequently asked questions. The original came in two finishes, gloss and matte. After these two classics were born, the Mod Podge people thought, "What if we developed different formulas for specific needs?" So they did. Even though some of the properties of the newer formulas overlap the originals, Mod Podge kept the classic gloss and matte and simply expanded their line.

No matter which you choose, remember that all Mod Podge formulas can do the same three things—gluing, sealing, and finishing. Also keep in mind that all Mod Podge is self-sealing. You don't need to spray it with acrylic sealer, but I sometimes recommend it for added durability for projects that will get frequent use.

CLASSIC

This formula comes in two finishes, gloss and matte; when dry, gloss has a shiny finish and matte does not. When I hear crafters' feedback on the gloss formula, it's typically, "After it's dry, it's sticky." Sometimes I hear that about matte, too. However, there's a very simple solution. Just spray the surface with several coats of a clear acrylic sealer, and you'll be fine. Stickiness will vanish, and you'll also gain extra layers of protection.

Result: Great for all types of projects and most surfaces. This is your all-around Mod Podge.

SATIN

This first cousin to the gloss and matte formulas has a finish somewhere in between the two, providing you with a lustrous, soft appearance. Because it's oh-so-slightly frosted, it shows scratches less than matte or gloss.

Result: Perfect for projects where you want a non-glossy, soft appearance that wears well.

HARD COAT

This formula was specially developed for furniture and other functional pieces to provide extra protection for projects that you use and handle frequently. It has a satin finish so it doesn't show the scratches like the matte or gloss.

Result: A must when working with furniture. It's the ultimate, durable Mod Podge finish.

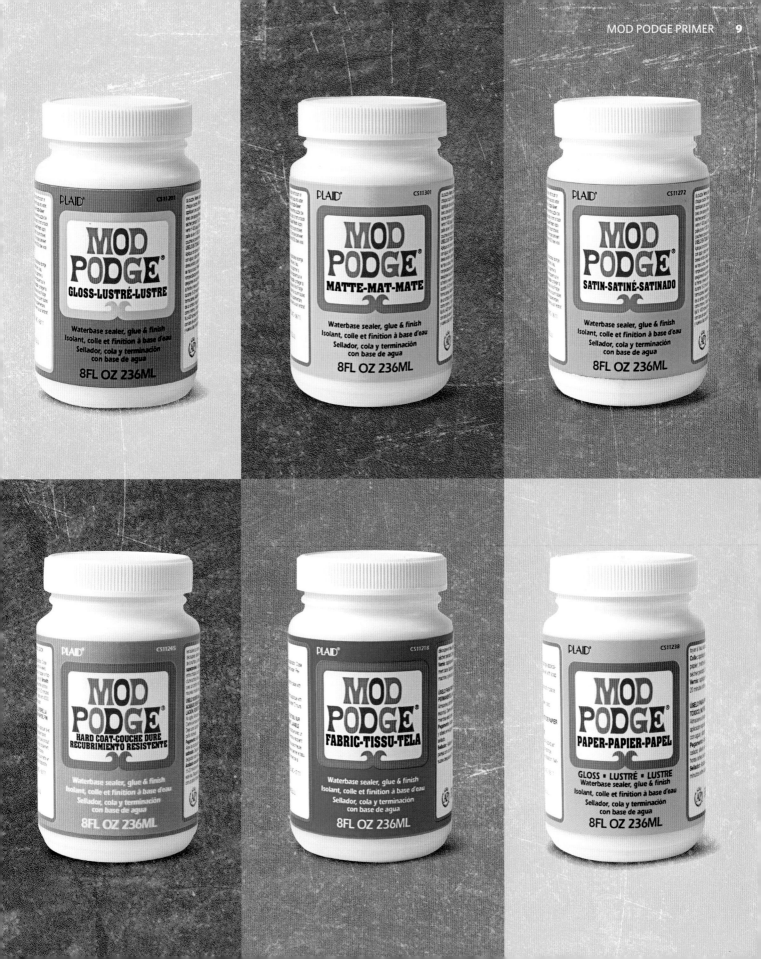

FABRIC

Along with paper and wood, people love to decoupage on fabric. Not only that, I love to decoupage fabric to other surfaces. This formula allows you to do both. Just lightly brush it on the fabric and let it dry before cutting. Fabric Mod Podge prevents the fabric from fraying.

Result: Use this formula to prepare fabric for decoupaging to surfaces and for decoupaging onto fabric.

PAPER

This formula confuses a lot of people who ask, "Can't you just use regular Mod Podge for paper?" The answer is yes, but here's the real reason. The Mod Podge people developed this special archival formula for crafters who do more advanced paper projects, including scrapbooking.

Result: Archival in quality, it keeps photos and papers from yellowing, and extends the life of scrapbooking projects. Comes in both a gloss and matte finish.

OUTDOOR

Decoupage + stuff that goes outdoors = Outdoor Mod Podge. It protects your projects from moisture and the elements and is great for everything outdoors, including clay pots, birdhouses, and wall art.

Result: Use it for everything decoupaged that will sit outside. I recommend also sealing projects with an outdoor sealer for added durability.

SPARKLE

Craving more sparkle and shine—who isn't? This formula has bling already in it. Sparkle has a hologram glitter for a rainbow effect. Use several coats for even more glitz.

Result: Makes projects glimmer. Dark surfaces highlight the sparkle even more.

DIMENSIONAL MAGIC

Just as the name implies, this formula will magically add new dimensions to your projects. It is thicker than other formulas and dries crystal clear.

Result: Use it to raise areas or embellishments on your design to new heights. When making jewelry, a layer or two seals motifs into any component with raised sides.

Basic Techniques

Please read these instructions thoroughly for hassle-free Mod Podging. There are six steps from start to finish. I promise if you follow them, you'll end up with a great project and be a very happy Podger! *Note:* After you've applied a coat of Mod Podge, let it dry before you add another one or before you move to the next step. Once you've completed your project, always allow it to dry for 24 to 48 hours before using.

1. PREPARE THE SURFACE

You can decoupage almost any surface. Appropriate surfaces include wood, papier-mâché, terra cotta, tin, cardboard, glass, and craft foam. Note that only some plastics are suitable for decoupage—I recommend testing a small area before starting your project to make sure that the Mod Podge will adhere.

Glass, tin, and wood need extra attention in their preparation. When working with glass, remove surface oils by washing and drying it with a lint-free cloth. For older tin, clean it with a 50/50 vinegar and water solution, and use a wire brush on any stubborn rust spots. Sand unfinished wood surfaces with a fine-grit sandpaper until smooth. Fill any holes with wood putty, and sand again. Wipe clean, using a tack cloth or damp paper towel to remove any dust from sanding.

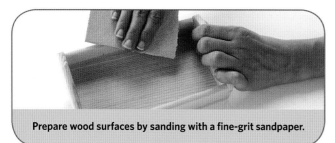
Prepare wood surfaces by sanding with a fine-grit sandpaper.

All other surfaces can be decoupaged without any preparation, although you should always make sure the surface you're working with is clean and dirt free. It's not necessary, but some crafters like to paint the prepared surface with acrylic paints before applying the Mod Podge.

If you want, you can paint unfinished surfaces with acrylic paint.

2. PREPARE THE MATERIALS

You can Mod Podge most materials as-is, especially thicker papers. Here are a few tips about preparing common materials before you begin.

Fabric

Wash and dry the fabric (do not use fabric softener). Iron, and then lay the fabric on a covered work surface—using wax paper to cover your table is preferable. Use a brush to paint a light coat of Fabric Mod Podge onto your fabric.

Apply a thin layer onto the fabric.

Allow the fabric to dry. This will enable you to cut the fabric like paper without worrying about frayed edges.

Notice the clean, unfrayed edges when cutting prepared fabric.

Paper

If you're working with thinner sheets of scrapbook paper, you may find it helpful to spray your paper with a clear acrylic sealer before Mod Podging. Spray both sides and allow to dry before decoupaging. An alternative method is to use a spray bottle with water to spritz the paper before immediately smoothing it down on a Mod Podged surface.

You don't need to prepare tissue paper, but you need to know that it is very difficult to Mod Podge it without wrinkles. The good news is you can embrace those wrinkles since they add charm and a little character to your surface. When Mod Podging tissue paper, work slowly so that it doesn't tear.

3. PLAN YOUR DESIGN

Cut out your paper or the other material(s) you're planning to decoupage. Experiment with design elements to determine the layout of your piece. Add interest to your design by using large and small pieces, layering and overlapping elements and coordinating colors.

4. ADHERE YOUR MATERIALS

Use the Mod Podge formula of choice to adhere each component to your surface. Always start with the underlying design elements and work your way upward. Apply a medium coat of Mod Podge to the surface. Be aware that if you use too little Mod Podge, you'll get wrinkles. It's better to apply more than less—you can always wipe away any excess with a paintbrush. For very small elements, brush adhesive onto the project surface, and use tweezers to apply each piece.

In this case, more is best! Too little Mod Podge, and you'll get wrinkles.

Lay your material(s) or item(s) to be decoupaged on top of the Mod Podge, and use your hands to smooth thoroughly. Keep smoothing until you remove all bubbles.

When working with large pieces, smooth from the center outward. You can also use a squeegee or brayer to remove air bubbles. Use the squeegee with smaller items such as trays—it's perfect for getting into corners—and the brayer on larger flat surfaces. Once you've finished smoothing the materials, use your brush to wipe away any excess Mod Podge. Allow the piece to dry for no less than 15 to 20 minutes before moving to the next step.

Mod Podge Tool Kit

You'll always need these items on hand for any project. Gather them early and keep them in one place. Nothing's worse than searching for something when you're in the middle of the creative flow. Each project will always tell you what Mod Podge formula(s) to use.

Mod Podge, formula(s) specified

Mod Podge Tool Set,
includes one squeegee and one brayer

Paper towels

Disposable foam plates or palette

Scissors

Craft knife and self-sealing mat

Water basin

Brushes for applying Mod Podge
(disposable foam works well)

Paintbrushes

Craft glue

Ruler

Tape measure

Pencil or pen

Sandpaper in a variety of grits

Steel wool, extra-fine to fine

The squeegee from the Mod Podge Tool Set is perfect for smoothing in tight spaces.

Use a brayer for larger items such as furniture.

5. SEAL THE PROJECT

Use a foam brush, sponge, or flat brush to apply the final protective coat of Mod Podge to your project. Allow to dry, and then repeat. You can finish with one coat, but I always recommend applying at least two.

One coat will do to finish, but two or more are always better for added durability.

For a very smooth finish, wet a piece of #400-grit sandpaper with water and sand lightly between finishing coats. Before applying the final coat, wipe the surface dry after sandpapering, and then polish with #0000 steel wool. To avoid tackiness, use a clear acrylic spray.

Sand between finishing coats for an even smoother surface.

6. ADD EMBELLISHMENTS

Once your project is dry, add embellishments as desired. Adhere them with a suitable adhesive such as hot glue, craft glue, or epoxy.

Have fun gluing embellishments to your project.

To create your own embellishments, or to add extra dimension to your project, use Dimensional Magic Mod Podge. It creates a raised surface that you can use on top of any Mod Podged or painted surface, and works especially well with jewelry.

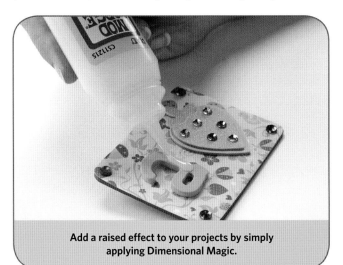

Add a raised effect to your projects by simply applying Dimensional Magic.

WEARABLES

A lot of crafters overlook Mod Podge when it comes to more delicate items like jewelry and accessories, but it's actually perfect for adding that extra touch to make a project beautiful. Dimensional Magic is especially useful for fashion items; if you've never used this amazing formula, you're going to be hooked. Use Mod Podge and Dimensional Magic together and you'll have people asking you, "Where did you get that?"

MOD PODGE® ROCKS!

MOD BOOTS

One of the projects that my blog readers get the most excited about is Mod Podged shoes. Yes, you can actually Mod Podge shoes and wear them! The only tip I have for you (besides picking fun fabric) is to apply a clear acrylic spray sealer when done for extra protection. They won't be totally waterproof—so no dancing in puddles no matter how tempted you are.

WHAT YOU'LL NEED   MOD PODGE TOOL KIT (PAGE 13) ◼ FABRIC MOD PODGE ◼
FUN FABRIC OF CHOICE, AT LEAST ½ YARD (45.7 CM) OR ENOUGH TO COVER THE BOOTS ◼
PAPER TO MAKE A PATTERN ◼ SMOOTH PLEATHER OR LEATHER BOOTS

WHAT YOU DO

1   Prepare your fabric with the Fabric Mod Podge (page 12). Allow to dry.

2   Make a paper pattern for each boot Ⓐ. Tape the paper to the boot, and trace the areas with a pencil, making sure to add a little extra seam allowance to the back and zipper seams. Cut out the pattern pieces. Your pattern should have at least three pieces, one for the outside, and two for the inside with zipper.

3   Trace the pattern onto the backside of the prepared fabric, and cut out Ⓑ.

4   Working a small section at a time, brush Fabric Mod Podge onto the boot Ⓒ. Position the fabric on the Mod Podged area, and use your fingers to smooth out any air bubbles. Continue adhering the fabric in this manner. Trim any overhang with scissors.

5   Overlap the fabric on the back of the boot. Allow to dry and then add a second coat of Mod Podge over the fabric portion.

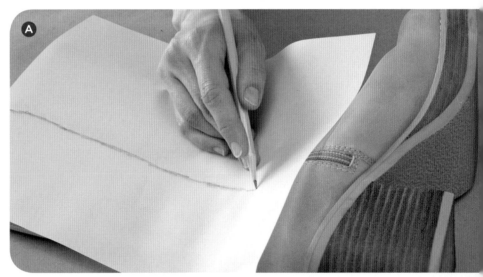

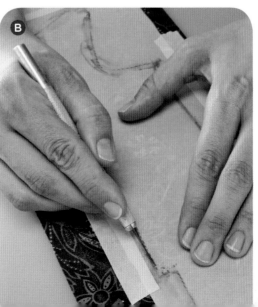

LOVE OF NATURE BELT BUCKLES

I used to think belt buckles were only for cowboys or country line dancers. Now I know a belt buckle can be whatever style you want it to be, especially if you use Mod Podge to make it! Look for belt buckles with high sides that create a well for your design surface. They're the kind you need when using Dimensional Magic Mod Podge. I found the buckles for this project on Etsy.

WHAT YOU'LL NEED   MOD PODGE TOOL KIT (PAGE 13)   ■   GLOSS MOD PODGE   ■
DIMENSIONAL MAGIC MOD PODGE   ■   SILVER BELT-BUCKLE BLANK WITH RAISED SIDES   ■
VELLUM   ■   REMOVABLE TAPE   ■   2 SMALL SHEETS OR SCRAPS OF SCRAPBOOK PAPER   ■
EMBELLISHMENTS OF CHOICE, SUCH AS BUTTONS, BRADS, RHINESTONES, OR GLITTER

WHAT YOU DO

1   Cut a rectangle of vellum to fit over the belt buckle.

2   With a pencil, trace the shape of the belt buckle on the vellum. Do this by holding the vellum firmly with one hand and rubbing the pencil around the belt buckle edge with the other. Use removable tape to secure if necessary.

3   Tape the vellum to the scrapbook paper, and trace around it. Use a craft knife to cut out the shape Ⓐ. Check the fit inside the belt buckle, and trim if necessary.

4   Apply the Gloss Mod Podge to the buckle, and then lay the cut paper on it. Smooth with your fingers to remove any bubbles and then allow to dry.

5   Place the embellishments on the belt buckle, and Mod Podge in place. Allow to dry Ⓑ. Apply Gloss Mod Podge to the buckle as a topcoat.

6   Apply a thin layer of Dimensional Magic into the bottom of the belt buckle Ⓒ. Let it dry for several hours before applying a second layer.
DESIGNER NOTE → *For a three-dimensional look, apply the first layer of Dimensional Magic to the buckle and let dry. Apply the second layer and lay your embellishments directly into the wet Dimensional Magic.*

7   Apply a third layer of Dimensional Magic to completely fill the well of the buckle. Depending on the depth of the well, you may need to apply more than three layers. Let it dry for at least 24 hours before wearing.
TIP → *Put items into Dimensional Magic immediately when wet for perfect results.*

PRESSED LEAF PENDANT

DESIGNER: **Candie Cooper**

Bet you didn't know I have a forestry degree. If you were to take a hike with me, I would chat your ear off about flowers, tree identification, or the habitat of slugs. I truly appreciate nature, and I like it when artists, like Candie, bring them into crafts and fashion. Pressed leaves add interest to jewelry, and they're also free. It doesn't get much better than that.

WHAT YOU'LL NEED MOD PODGE TOOL KIT (PAGE 13) ☐ GLOSS MOD PODGE ☐
DIMENSIONAL MAGIC MOD PODGE ☐ SMALL LEAVES ☐ DECORATIVE PAPER ☐
BEZEL PENDANT ☐ TWEEZERS (OPTIONAL) ☐ 8MM JUMP RING ☐ 1 YARD (.9 M)
LEATHER CORD ☐ BUTTON ☐ SMALL EMBELLISHMENTS (OPTIONAL)

WHAT YOU DO

1 Clip leaves from small house or outdoor plants, and press them between the pages of a book. Let them sit for a week or so before using them to make sure they're completely dried.

2 Cut the decorative paper to fit inside the bezel frame. Use the Gloss Mod Podge to adhere the paper to the frame, and then adhere the leaf to the paper Ⓐ. Allow to dry.

> **DESIGNER NOTE →** *When working small, it helps to use tweezers when positioning the leaf.*

3 Fill the frame with a layer of Dimensional Magic Mod Podge Ⓑ. Apply a second layer of Dimensional Magic once the first layer is dry.

4 Attach a jump ring to the loop on the pendant. Make a loop at one end of the cord with an overhand knot Ⓒ.

5 String the pendant onto the cord. Determine the desired length of the necklace, and add approximately 1 inch (2.5 cm).

6 String the button onto the cord so the cord goes through the backside of the button and down through the front. Make a knot at the end of the cord, and slide the button to the end.

7 If you wish, add small buttons, metal flowers, and other embellishments to the top layer of the pendant. Use a toothpick to apply craft glue to the backs of the embellishments—tweezers may come in handy here!

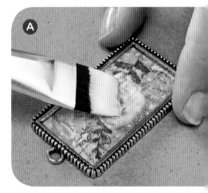

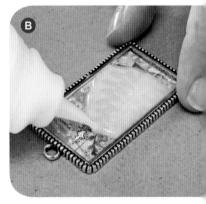

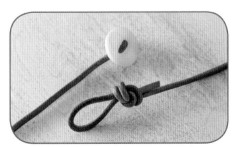

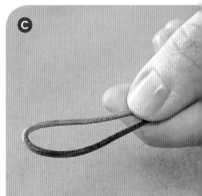

PAWS & FLOWERS SCREEN-PRINTED DOG COAT

I'm one of those people. I like to dress up my dogs in costumes. I swear my three little dogs love it because they always get a treat at the end. Okay, maybe they don't love it—but I think they're so willing because they know how happy it makes me. Here's how you can get in on some of that doggy-costume action using Mod Podge to make your screen.

WHAT YOU'LL NEED MOD PODGE TOOL KIT (PAGE 13) ☐ FABRIC MOD PODGE ☐ DESIGN, EITHER HAND DRAWN OR CLIP ART PRINTED FROM THE INTERNET ☐ SHEER FABRIC, AN OLD SHEER CURTAIN PANEL WORKS WELL ☐ EMBROIDERY HOOP ☐ COTTON DOG COAT ☐ BROWN FABRIC SCREEN-PRINTING INK ☐ FOAM DAUBER OR PAINTBRUSH

WHAT YOU DO

1 Pick out a design to screen-print. Draw the design by hand on a sheet of paper Ⓐ, or, print it out if you found your design online.
DESIGNER NOTE → *I selected paws and a bone for the motifs to go along with the dog's name.*

2 Fasten the sheer fabric into the embroidery hoop. Pull the fabric taut, and then screw the hoop closed.

3 Use scissors to cut the excess material from around the hoop. Turn the hoop over, place it over the design, and use a pencil to trace it directly onto the fabric Ⓑ.

4 Using a brush, paint the Fabric Mod Podge directly onto the sheer fabric (your screen) where you don't want the ink to go through Ⓒ. Apply several coats, allowing one coat to dry before applying the next one.

5 Once dry, place the screen on the dog coat. Lay old newspapers or plastic under the coat to prevent the ink from seeping through to your work surface.

PAWS & FLOWERS SCREEN-PRINTED DOG COAT

6 Use the foam dauber or paintbrush to apply the fabric screen-printing ink to the screen Ⓓ. Pay special attention to the corners of the motifs and letters.

7 Pull the screen up immediately after applying the ink, and allow the ink on the coat to dry.

8 If needed, use a smaller paintbrush with the ink to touch up any areas or to even out your design.

9 Allow the ink to dry for 24 hours. Follow the manufacturer's instructions for setting the ink on the fabric.

TIP → *You can use the screen several times. Wash it immediately after painting to optimize its life. If the Mod Podge wears away in certain areas after washing, simply apply more before the next use.*

Ⓒ

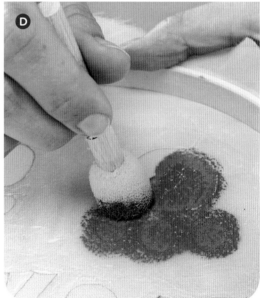

Ⓓ

CHILDREN'S ART CHARM BRACELET

Children's art is innocent, funny, and cute all at the same time. One of my most prized possessions is a hand-drawn book given to me by a second grade class where I volunteered. This bracelet is ever so much more charming because it uses children's art. Candie has created the perfect project for anyone looking to preserve those prized masterpieces.

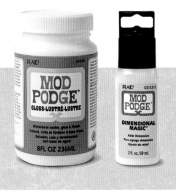

WHAT YOU'LL NEED   MOD PODGE TOOL KIT (PAGE 13)   ☐ GLOSS MOD PODGE   ☐ DIMENSIONAL MAGIC MOD PODGE   ☐ CHILDREN'S ARTWORK   ☐ LINKED-BRACELET BLANK WITH PICTURE-FRAME BEZELS   ☐ SQUARE TEMPLATE   ☐ DRY RICE(OPTIONAL)   ☐ BEAD ASSORTMENT (OPTIONAL)   ☐ CHARMS (OPTIONAL)   ☐ 4MM JUMP RINGS (OPTIONAL)   ☐ ROUND-NOSE PLIERS (OPTIONAL)

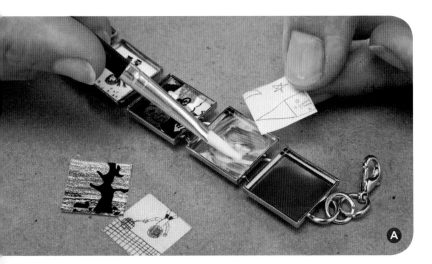

WHAT YOU DO

1   Use a copy machine to reduce the children's artwork to the desired size. You want it to fit inside the picture-frame bezels of the bracelet.

DESIGNER NOTE → *If the art is abstract, you could use sections of it for the entire bracelet.*

2   Cut the artwork to fit the bezel frames. Using a square template is helpful to get the size just right.

3   Glue each image inside the frames using the Gloss Mod Podge Ⓐ.

4   Fill each of the frames with a layer of Dimensional Magic Mod Podge, and allow to dry Ⓑ. Optionally, you can apply a second layer of Dimensional Magic once the first layer is dry.

DESIGNER NOTE → *If your bracelet doesn't lay level, pour some dry rice on a small plate, and pat flat. Lay the bracelet on top of the rice, and pat until the bracelet is level.*

BEADED DANGLES

Make your own beaded dangles. String beads onto a headpin. Leave enough of the wire un-beaded for wrapping. After beading, use round-nose pliers to bend the wire 45° just above the last bead. Insert the wire into a link in a necklace or bracelet, loop the wire around the link, and then wrap the excess wire a few times around the shaft of the headpin above the last bead. Use wire cutters to trim any excess wire.

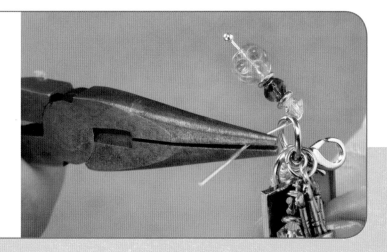

5   If you desire, you can add to the fun by embellishing the bracelet with beads and charms. Use the round-nose pliers to attach the embellishments to the bracelet with the jump rings.

DESIGNER NOTE → *Open the jump ring with the pliers from side to side, slip it into the hole in the embellishment, insert the jump ring in a link on the bracelet, and then close the ring securely.*

BOTTLE CAP
NECKLACE

DESIGNER: **Heather Mann**

Bottle caps aren't just for root beer anymore! Now you can make them into jewelry by Mod Podging decorative paper inside before filling them with Dimensional Magic. Use jump rings to attach them to a linked necklace, and you're ready to go to town. You'll find making these little gems addictive. Heather's project incorporates candy wrappers for some added fun.

WHAT YOU'LL NEED MOD PODGE TOOL KIT (PAGE 13) ☐ GLOSS MOD PODGE ☐ DIMENSIONAL MAGIC MOD PODGE ☐ ONE LARGE BOTTLE CAP ☐ SIX SMALL BOTTLE CAPS ☐ AWL ☐ CANDY WRAPPERS OF YOUR CHOICE ☐ LINKED NECKLACE WITH THREE STRANDS ☐ 4MM JUMP RINGS ☐ ROUND-NOSE PLIERS ☐ BEAD ASSORTMENT (OPTIONAL) ☐ CHARMS (OPTIONAL)

WHAT YOU DO

1 Use the awl to punch a hole in each bottle cap for attaching them to the necklace.

2 Cut candy wrappers to fit inside each of the bottle caps. You might find it helpful to make a circle template in the correct size to guide your cutting.

3 Use the Gloss Mod Podge to glue each wrapper inside their bottle-cap frames Ⓐ.

4 Fill each of the bottle caps with a layer of Dimensional Magic Mod Podge Ⓑ, and leave to dry. Optionally, you can add a second layer once the first layer is dry.

5 Use the round-nose pliers to attach the bottle caps to the necklace with the jump rings Ⓒ.
DESIGNER NOTE → *Open the jump ring with the pliers from side to side, slip it into the hole in the bottle cap, insert it in a link on the necklace, and then close the ring securely.*

6 (Optional) Attach charms and beaded dangles on the necklace if desired, using the jump rings as you did in step 5. See page 27 for more on making your own beaded dangles.

GIRL ABOUT TOWN
BIKE HELMET

If you're going to ride a bike, you should definitely do it in style. I believe in turning heads, and that's just what this helmet is designed to do (well, besides protecting your noggin). Even if you're a professional, I highly encourage you to stir things up a bit with this protective patchwork project.

WHAT YOU'LL NEED MOD PODGE TOOL KIT (PAGE 13) ◼ FABRIC MOD PODGE ◼
OUTDOOR MOD PODGE ◼ FABRIC SCRAPS, ENOUGH TO COVER THE HELMET ◼
BICYCLE HELMET ◼ OUTDOOR ACRYLIC SPRAY SEALER (OPTIONAL)

WHAT YOU DO

1 Prepare the fabric with Fabric Mod Podge (page 12). Allow to dry.

2 Cut rectangles of various sizes from the fabric scraps, cutting enough to cover the helmet Ⓐ.

3 Use the Outdoor Mod Podge to glue the rectangles one by one onto the helmet Ⓑ. Since helmets come in different shapes, you may need to trim around certain areas to fit.

4 Cover the entire surface of the helmet with Outdoor Mod Podge as a finish, and allow to dry.

5 Apply two coats of Outdoor Mod Podge as a sealer. Allow the first coat to dry before applying the second.

6 (Optional) Spray the helmet with an acrylic sealer suitable for outdoor use to make it more water resistant.

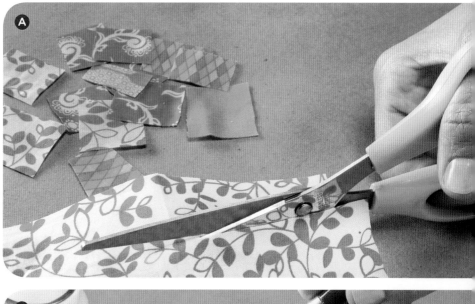

BRIGHT BEADED WOODEN BANGLES

Bangle bracelets are my go-to project when I need a gift. Everyone loves them (if I do say so myself), and you can customize them with paint, paper, and embellishments that you already have in your stash. These wooden bracelets work up quickly and will look great using any type of Mod Podge formula. I used five-sided bangles with raised ovals, but you can adapt the project when using any wide wooden bangle.

WHAT YOU'LL NEED   MOD PODGE TOOL KIT (PAGE 13) ▪ GLOSS MOD PODGE ▪
DIMENSIONAL MAGIC MOD PODGE ▪ 2 FIVE-SIDED WOODEN BANGLES WITH RAISED OVALS ▪
1 SMALL SHEET OF VELLUM ▪ PAINTER'S TAPE ▪ 2 SHEETS OR SCRAPS OF SCRAPBOOK PAPER ▪
ACRYLIC CRAFT PAINT IN TEAL AND YELLOW-GREEN ▪ MICROBEADS

WHAT YOU DO

1   Cut a small square of vellum to fit over each oval on the bracelets (for this project, I cut five squares for each bracelet).

2   Make a tracing of each oval on the squares. Do this by holding the vellum firmly with one hand and rubbing the pencil around the shape with the other Ⓐ. Use tape to secure if necessary.

3   Tape the vellum to the scrapbook paper or scraps, and cut out using scissors or a craft knife Ⓑ. Check the fit on the ovals, and trim if necessary. Set aside.

4   Paint one bracelet teal and the other yellow-green using the acrylic paint. Apply three coats each, allowing each coat to dry before applying the next one. Allow to dry.

5   Use the Gloss Mod Podge to glue the cut scrapbook paper onto the ovals around each bracelet. Allow to dry, and then apply a topcoat of the Gloss Mod Podge on each.

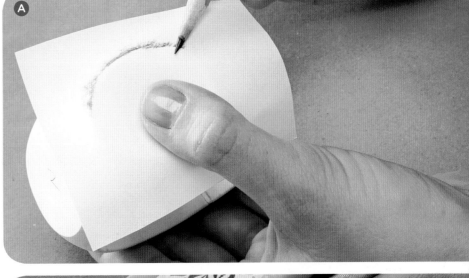

6 Use craft glue to run a thin line of glue around the edge of one of the paper ovals. Sprinkle the microbeads on the glue, and allow to dry Ⓒ. Work around each bracelet, allowing each line of glue and beads to dry before moving on to the next. When dry, the line of glue and beads will create a shallow well inside each oval.

7 Apply a layer of Dimensional Magic in each well, filling them halfway Ⓓ. Allow to dry for several hours, and then apply another layer to fill the wells all the way. Let dry for at least 24 hours before wearing.

HOME DÉCOR

No well-decorated living space is complete without a few stylish Mod Podge projects. Decoupage brings out the designer in everyone. From bookshelves to footstools and wall art to chairs, there is nothing in your house that should be safe from your brush and bottle. Mod Podge is perfect for refurbishing items and giving them a second life in your home.

MOD PODGE® ROCKS!

CRAZY FOR FALL PAINTED ACORNS

While looking for a fall display idea about a year ago, I decided I would use up some blue and brown paint by painting acorns I found outside the place I worked. I learned that people like acorns—a lot. That project quickly became the most popular project of all time on my blog. For this project, I used wooden acorns, which are great because they don't have the worm beasties that live inside the natural variety. Paint these in the palette of your choice, whatever makes you happy or goes with your décor.

WHAT YOU'LL NEED   MOD PODGE TOOL KIT (PAGE 13)   ▪ DIMENSIONAL MAGIC MOD PODGE   ▪ SPARKLE MOD PODGE (OPTIONAL)   ▪ WOODEN ACORNS, AS MANY AS NEEDED FOR YOUR DISPLAY   ▪ ACRYLIC CRAFT PAINT IN MAGENTA AND DARK PINK, OR COLORS OF YOUR CHOICE   ▪ WAX PAPER   ▪ GLASS CONTAINER FOR DISPLAY

WHAT YOU DO

1   Paint the base of your acorns using the magenta acrylic paint, or color of your choice Ⓐ.

   DESIGNER NOTE → *You can also go with the traditional acorn colors: red-brown for the bottom; dark brown for the cap. Apply several coats, allowing each coat to dry before applying the next one.*

2   Paint the tops of your acorns using the dark pink acrylic paint, or color of your choice. Apply several coats, allowing each coat to dry before applying the next one.

3   Place all of your painted acorns on wax paper. Drizzle Dimensional Magic Mod Podge over them one at a time Ⓑ. Cover one side of the acorns, and allow to dry before turning them over to cover the other side.

4   Allow to dry for 24 hours before placing them in the glass container.

   VARIATION → *Add some sparkle! Apply Sparkle Mod Podge to the painted acorns, allow to dry, and then apply the Dimensional Magic Mod Podge. If you're in a holiday mood, use Sparkle Mod Podge with gold or silver glitter.*

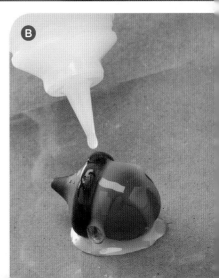

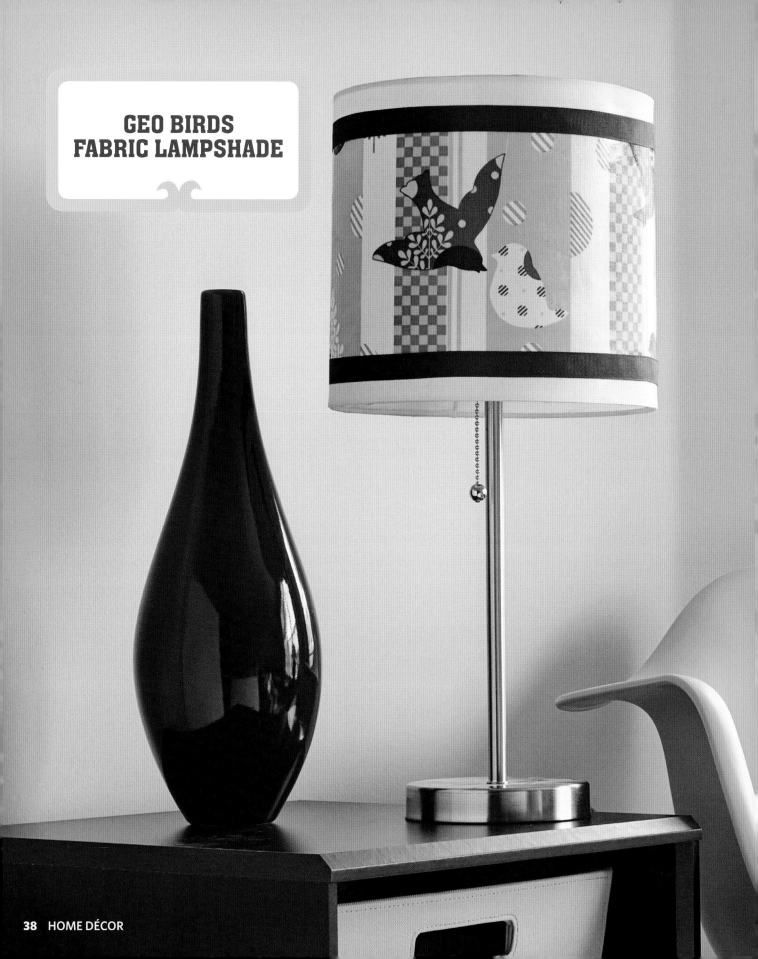

GEO BIRDS FABRIC LAMPSHADE

Do you have an old or plain lamp that you just can't look at anymore? Good. Then all you need is a piece of fabric, ribbon, and Mod Podge to make it terrifically un-boring. Customize to a room's décor or just go crazy with what you have—kind of like I did. This project is great for beginners, and makes a big statement in any room.

WHAT YOU'LL NEED   MOD PODGE TOOL KIT (PAGE 13) ◼ FABRIC MOD PODGE ◼ FABRIC, ENOUGH TO FIT AROUND THE LAMP SHADE ◼ ROUND LAMP SHADE IN ANY SIZE ◼ ROTARY CUTTER AND MAT (OPTIONAL) ◼ 2 YARDS (1.8 M) OF BROWN GROSGRAIN RIBBON ◼ HOT GLUE GUN AND GLUE STICKS

WHAT YOU DO

1   Prepare your fabric using the Fabric Mod Podge (page 12) Ⓐ. Allow to dry.

2   Remove the lamp shade from the base of the lamp, and carefully measure around it for size.

3   Use scissors or a rotary cutter (if you have one), and ruler to cut a strip of fabric to fit around the lamp shade.

4   Carefully Mod Podge the fabric to the lamp shade Ⓑ. Starting at the lamp shade seam, Mod Podge approximately 4 inches (10.2 cm) of fabric at a time, applying Mod Podge and smoothing the fabric as you go.

5   Finish the fabric wrap by slightly overlapping the fabric at the seam. Trim if necessary and allow to dry.

6   Add a topcoat of Mod Podge over the entire lamp shade to seal. Allow to dry.

7   Use the hot glue to adhere the ribbon to the edge of the fabric all around the lamp shade Ⓒ. Allow to dry for 24 hours before using.

TIP → *Take it a step further. Cut motifs from favorite print fabrics to create a pretty collage. Apply them to the fabric either during step 1 or before applying the topcoat in step 6.*

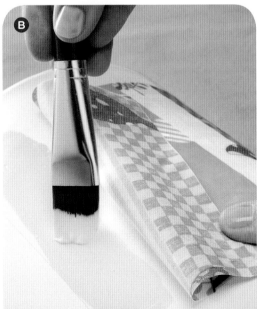

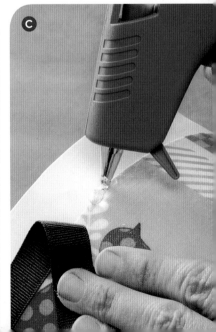

GNOME WALL PLAQUE

DESIGNER: *Holli Long*

I'm lucky to have a lot of friends that understand my love of garden gnomes, and Holli is one of them. Did you know these figurines originated in 19th century Germany? It's not really official, but I consider them to be good luck. This little guy can grace your front door, a sunroom, or even a garden—but remember to use Outdoor Mod Podge for the last one!

WHAT YOU'LL NEED MOD PODGE TOOL KIT (PAGE 13) ■ GLOSS MOD PODGE ■ 3 FEET (.9 M) OF DECORATIVE WOODEN MOLDING ■ WOODEN SIGN ■ ACRYLIC PAINT IN LIGHT PURPLE, GREEN, BLACK, LIGHT GOLDEN BROWN, AND IVORY ■ PARAFFIN WAX ■ GNOME IMAGE ■ CRAFT KNIFE ■ HOT GLUE GUN AND GLUE STICKS

WHAT YOU DO

1 Measure and cut the wooden molding to fit as the outer border of the sign. Use craft glue to attach the molding to the sign.

2 Use the black acrylic paint to paint the molding and wooden sign, and allow to dry completely.

3 Rub the paraffin wax over the painted surfaces.

4 Paint the molding with green and light purple. Paint the face of the sign with light golden brown, mixing some of the ivory paint into the brushstrokes as you go. Paint the outer edge of the sign light purple. Allow to dry.

5 To create the distressed look, lightly sand the surfaces with fine-grit sandpaper until the black comes through the topcoat of paint Ⓐ.

6 Make five color copies of your chosen gnome image. Coat the front and back of each copy with the Gloss Mod Podge, and allow to dry. Use scissors to cut out the first image, and Mod Podge it to the center of the painted sign Ⓑ.

7 Cut out the remaining images with a craft knife.

> **DESIGNER NOTE** → *If desired, you can use a craft knife to separate the pieces of the images, such as hat, face, shirt, pants, and legs before gluing as layers.*

8 Layer the images, applying drops of hot glue between layers Ⓒ. Hold each layer down with some light pressure to keep it in place until the hot glue cools.

VINTAGE CHILDREN'S BOOK MIRROR

DESIGNER: *Julie Lewis*

Everyone has a favorite children's book that they remember. Mine was *Benjamin's 365 Birthdays* by Judi Barrett. Benjamin wrapped up his own things and gave them to himself, much like I do with my Mod Podge projects. Kidding! However, as Julie reminds us, it's wonderful whenever a fond memory can work its way into a project. If you can't bear to cut up a children's book, simply make color copies.

WHAT YOU'LL NEED   MOD PODGE TOOL KIT (PAGE 13)   ◻   GLOSS MOD PODGE   ◻
CIRCULAR WOODEN PICTURE FRAME   ◻   1 SHEET OF SCRAPBOOK PAPER   ◻
ACRYLIC CRAFT PAINT IN BROWN AND REDDISH BROWN   ◻   SEVERAL PAGES FROM A CHILDREN'S
BOOK   ◻   CIRCLE TEMPLATES IN VARIOUS SIZES   ◻   1-INCH (2.5 CM) CIRCLE PUNCH   ◻   10 OR MORE
COORDINATING BUTTONS   ◻   24 INCHES (61 CM) OF BURLAP TWINE   ◻   6-INCH-DIAMETER (15.2 CM)
ROUND MIRROR   ◻   HOT GLUE GUN AND GLUE STICKS

WHAT YOU DO

1   Place the frame face down on the scrapbook paper.

2   Use a pencil to make a tracing of the large circle on the outside of the picture frame and the smaller circle on the inside Ⓐ.

3   Measure in ½ inch (1.3 cm) from the inner and outer edges of the circle, and then use a pencil to mark. Trim the circle along the edges, using the marks as your guide. Set aside.

4   Paint the circular frame. Use the darker shade to paint the outside edge of the circle, and the lighter shade to paint the inside edge that will be next to the mirror. Apply at least two coats, allowing each coat to dry before applying the next.

5   While the frame is drying, use the circle templates to cut various sizes of circles from the pages of a children's book.

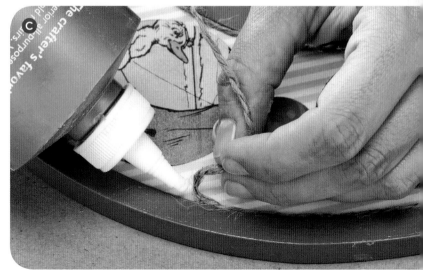

Cut at least eight circles. Use the 1-inch (2.5 cm) circle punch to punch out eight circles from the pages. Set aside.

6 Center the cutout scrapbook paper on the painted circular frame. Use a medium layer of the Gloss Mod Podge to glue the paper to the frame. Allow to dry. Apply a second finishing coat of Mod Podge, and let dry.

7 Mod Podge the 1-inch (2.5 cm) circles to the frame Ⓑ. Let dry, and then apply a final coat of Mod Podge to the front of the frame as a topcoat. Allow to dry.

8 Give the entire frame, front and back, a coat of Mod Podge. Allow to dry, then embellish the frame as desired using craft glue to attach the buttons and burlap twine Ⓒ.

9 Use hot glue to attach the mirror at the back of the frame. Allow to dry for 24 hours before hanging.

MISS MATCHY GLASS CANISTERS

Are you a matchy-matchy kitchen person? Actually, it doesn't matter with these canisters. You can match them perfectly or not—it's really up to you. Glass canisters are useful all over the house, but especially in the kitchen or pantry. Decorate as many as you need to hold your most important ingredients.

WHAT YOU'LL NEED MOD PODGE TOOL KIT (PAGE 13) ☐ GLOSS MOD PODGE ☐ THREE SIZES OF GLASS CONTAINERS WITH SCREW-ON LIDS AND FLAT SIDES ☐ SPRAY PAINT IN COLOR OF CHOICE ☐ 5 SHEETS OF DOUBLE-SIDED SCRAPBOOK PAPER ☐ CORNER-ROUNDING PUNCH ☐ 3 DECORATIVE KNOBS ☐ ADHESIVE-BACK LETTERS TO SPELL FLOUR, SUGAR, AND TEA ☐ 12 COORDINATING BUTTONS

WHAT YOU DO

1 Unscrew the lids from your containers, and spray paint them in a color of your choice. Apply two coats, allowing the first to dry before applying the second.

2 Carefully measure the flat sides of your containers, and cut the scrapbook paper to fit. Cut a front and back for each container. Use the corner-rounder punch to trim the corners on each piece.

3 Use the Gloss Mod Podge to glue the cut and trimmed paper to one of the flat sides of a container Ⓐ. Use a brayer to smooth and remove any bubbles and a paintbrush to wipe away any excess Mod Podge. Repeat on the opposite side of the container.

4 Repeat step 3 for the remaining containers. Allow to dry.

5 Apply two topcoats of Mod Podge to each container. Allow the first coat to dry before applying the second Ⓑ.

6 Glue the knobs to the lids of the jars. On the front of each container, use craft glue to glue the letters and button embellishments to the paper labels Ⓒ. Allow to dry for 24 hours before using.

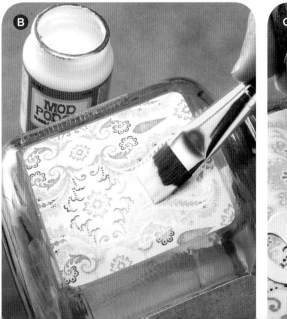

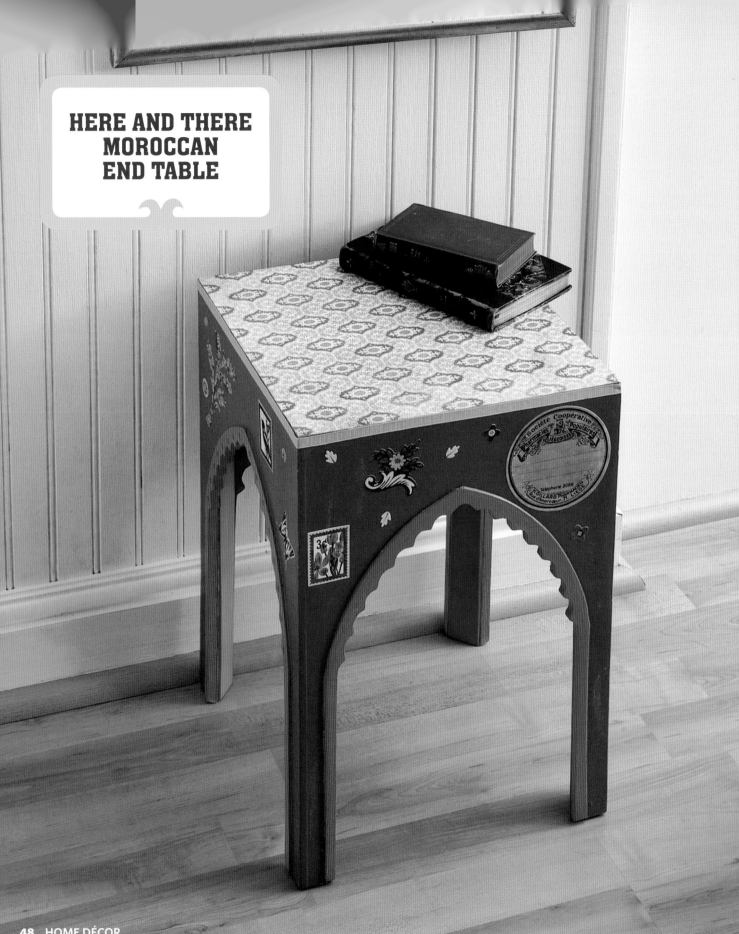

HERE AND THERE MOROCCAN END TABLE

I completely romanticize Morocco, even though I've never been there and really don't know anything about it. I spotted this table with scalloped trim at a thrift store, and the word "Moroccan" immediately came to mind. When I brought it home, I dressed it up to fit my thoughts of Morocco. Whether they're accurate or not, I love the results. Distressing the surface lends a hint of a mysterious past.

WHAT YOU'LL NEED MOD PODGE TOOL KIT (PAGE 13) ▪ HARD COAT MOD PODGE ▪ SMALL END TABLE ▪ TACK CLOTH OR PAPER TOWELS ▪ ACRYLIC PAINT IN AQUA, ORANGE, AND BRIGHT GREEN ▪ BEESWAX OR WHITE CANDLE ▪ SCRAPBOOK PAPER TO COVER THE TABLETOP ▪ SCRAPBOOK STICKERS TO COORDINATE WITH PAPER

WHAT YOU DO

1 Use a fine-grit sandpaper to prepare the surface. After sanding, use a paper towel or tack cloth to remove any dust.

2 Paint the entire table, with the exception of the trim, using the aqua acrylic paint. Apply several coats, allowing each coat to dry in between applications.

3 Rub the beeswax or candle over random areas of the table—wherever you want the aqua paint to show through. The more areas you wax, the more options you have for distressing. Set the beeswax or candle aside.

4 Paint the entire table, with the exception of the trim, using the bright green paint. Paint over the aqua and wax layers. Apply several coats, allowing each coat to dry in between applications.

5 Paint the trim with the orange acrylic paint, and allow to dry.

6 Use the sandpaper to sand the areas where you applied the wax Ⓐ. You'll see the aqua paint show through the bright green. Do not sand too deeply or you'll get to the original

wood surface. Sand as many areas as you want to get the amount of distressing you desire. Wipe away any dust.

7 Use the Hard Coat Mod Podge to glue the scrapbook paper to the top of the table. Smooth out air bubbles with your fingers, and finish smoothing by using the brayer Ⓑ. Allow to dry for 15 to 20 minutes.

8 Mod Podge the scrapbook stickers to the sides of the table Ⓒ. Allow to dry.

9 Apply a topcoat of Hard Coat Mod Podge to the entire table. Allow to dry, and then apply a second coat. Allow to dry 24 hours before using.

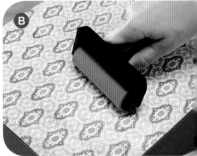

GEEK PLATES

Let's face it—I'm a geek. If you've read my blog, you know I wear glasses, love Star Wars, and have an undergrad degree in science. I also love to talk about statistics. It's definitely possible that I'll throw a nerd party some day, and now I'll have the plates all ready. Come to think of it, these plates would be a great addition to any party, and they're food-safe because you decoupage the backs.

WHAT YOU'LL NEED MOD PODGE TOOL KIT (PAGE 13) ☐ FABRIC MOD PODGE ☐
GLOSS MOD PODGE ☐ GLASS PLATES ☐ PRINTOUTS OF GEEKY DESIGNS ☐ TAPE ☐
ENAMEL GLASS PAINT IN SILVER AND AQUA ☐ FABRIC IN TWO DIFFERENT PRINTS,
½ YARD (45.7 CM) EACH

WHAT YOU DO

1 Look for geek-themed clip art on the web. Print out two designs of your choice. Make sure they'll fit in the centers of your plates. Tape the printouts to the fronts of the plates, cutting any excess around them to fit.

2 Use the printouts as guides to paint the designs on the back of each plate using the enamel paint and a small round paintbrush Ⓐ. Apply several coats, following the manufacturer's instructions for drying and setting the paint.

3 Prepare the fabric using the Fabric Mod Podge (page 12). Allow to dry.

4 Once the fabric is dry, cut into small squares Ⓑ. Make enough to cover the backs of the plates.

5 Use the Gloss Mod Podge to apply the fabric squares to the backs of the plates. Continue applying Mod Podge and squares, overlapping as you go Ⓒ. Work until the backs of the plates are completely covered. Allow to dry.

6 Use scissors to trim any excess fabric from around the plates.

7 Apply two coats of Gloss Mod Podge to the backs of the plates as the finish coat. Allow the first coat to dry before applying the second. Let dry for 24 hours before using.

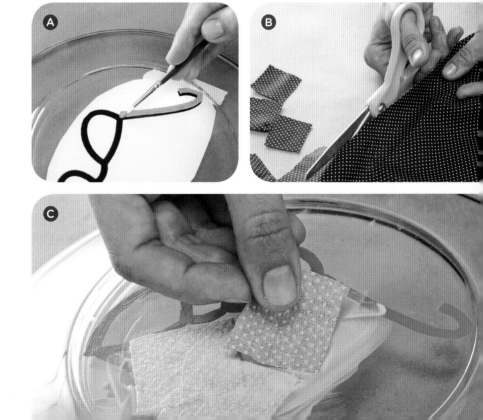

CARNIVAL RIBBON & TICKET FRAME

One of my current obsessions is using state fair ribbons and raffle tickets. They make me feel like I've won something, and who isn't happy about that? I went outside the box using this color palette (at least for myself), and really like the results. Putting an initial in the center of the ribbon lets you make the perfect personalized gift for any winner in your life.

WHAT YOU'LL NEED   MOD PODGE TOOL KIT (PAGE 13)   ■   MATTE MOD PODGE   ■   WOODEN FRAME THAT HOLDS A 3½ X 5-INCH (8.9 X 12.7 CM) PHOTO   ■   SCREWDRIVER   ■   2 SHEETS OF COORDINATING DOUBLE-SIDED SCRAPBOOK PAPER   ■   PATTERN FOR A RIBBON, OR (OPTIONAL) A RIBBON CUT FROM A DIE CUTTER   ■   ACRYLIC PAINT IN LIGHT PINK AND PEACH   ■   WOODEN LETTER   ■   2 FEET (61 CM) OF RAFFLE TICKETS CUT FROM A ROLL

WHAT YOU DO

1   Use a screwdriver, if needed, to remove the hardware and glass from the frame. Set aside.

2   Place the frame on the back of one sheet of the double-sided scrapbook paper. Trace around the outside and inside of the frame. Trim the paper to fit.

3   Go online to select a ribbon pattern that you like and print it out. Use the pattern to cut out a ribbon from the second sheet of scrapbook paper. If you have a die cutter, use it to cut a ribbon shape. Set your paper items aside.

4   Paint the frame light pink and the wooden letter peach. When the letter is dry, apply a coat of the Matte Mod Podge to seal, and allow to dry.

5   Apply a medium layer of Mod Podge to the frame Ⓐ, and lay the paper down on top of it. Make sure you carefully align the paper to the frame. Smooth the paper with your fingers to remove any air bubbles and allow to dry for 15 to 20 minutes.

6   Mod Podge the raffle tickets to the frame, starting on the horizontal plane of the frame Ⓑ. Repeat on the vertical side and trim any excess with a craft knife.

7   Return to your cutout state fair ribbon, and cut out the center. Flip the center to the other side of the paper for contrast. Apply Mod Podge to the ribbon, and allow to dry.

8   Use craft glue to adhere the ribbon and the wooden letter to the frame. Allow to dry for 24 hours before using.

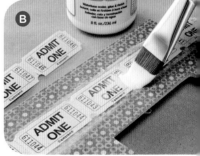

ZIGZAG ATOMIC MAILBOX

DESIGNER: *Julie Lewis*

My mind wanders to a pretty scenario...The local mailman walks up the step of a picturesque home and places the mail (no bills, just handwritten letters) into the Mod Podged mailbox. While he's depositing the letters, he thinks to himself what a wonderfully talented person must live here—how crafty, how creative.

WHAT YOU'LL NEED   MOD PODGE TOOL KIT (PAGE 13)   ■   OUTDOOR MOD PODGE   ■   METAL MAILBOX   ■
1 SHEET OF SCRAPBOOK PAPER   ■   CARDSTOCK IN BLACK, ORANGE, AND WHITE   ■   ZIGZAG DECORATIVE-EDGE
SCISSORS   ■   DIE CUTTER (OPTIONAL) OR TEMPLATE FOR LETTERS AND SHAPES   ■   1-INCH (2.5 CM) CIRCLE PUNCH

WHAT YOU DO

1   Carefully measure the front of the mailbox. Trim the scrapbook paper to fit, leaving at least a 1-inch (2.5 cm) border on all sides.

2   With the decorative-edge scissors, cut two zigzag strips from the orange cardstock (A).

3   Use a die cutter (B) (optional) or a template to cut out the letters M, A, I, and L from the black cardstock. Cut decorative frames to frame the letters from the black cardstock.

4   Punch four circles from the white cardstock with the 1-inch (2.5 cm) circle punch.

5   Apply a medium layer of the Outdoor Mod Podge to the front of the mailbox. Make sure the scrapbook paper is centered before laying it on the mailbox. Use your fingers to smooth out any air bubbles. Brush a layer of Mod Podge over the paper (C), and allow to dry for 15 to 20 minutes.

6   Mod Podge the zigzag strips, spacing them evenly at the top and bottom of the scrapbook paper. Allow to dry.

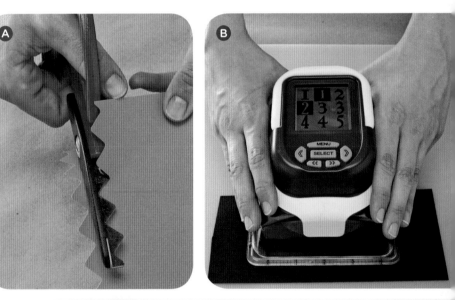

7 Spacing them evenly, Mod Podge the letters, circles, and decorative frames on the top of the scrapbook paper 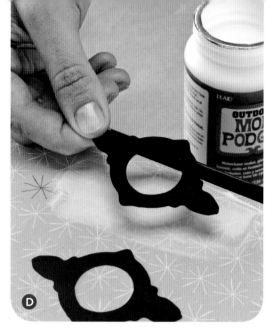(D). Allow to dry.

8 Apply two coats of Outdoor Mod Podge to the front of the mailbox, allowing the first coat to dry before applying the second. Allow to dry for 24 hours before using.

MODERN CHAIRS MEDIA TOWER

I enjoy interesting fabric. I also enjoy the irony of putting a chair print on a media tower. Of course, you can use any print of choice. When making the stencils, simply select a motif that reflects the print. Then, when you remove the stored media, you'll always have a nice little surprise waiting for you.

WHAT YOU'LL NEED MOD PODGE TOOL KIT (PAGE 13) ◼ FABRIC MOD PODGE ◼ HARD COAT MOD PODGE ◼ UNFINISHED WOODEN MEDIA TOWER ◼ TACK CLOTH OR PAPER TOWELS ◼ WHITE ACRYLIC PAINT ◼ 1 YARD (.9 M) OF FABRIC IN PRINT OF CHOICE ◼ TWO COLORS OF ACRYLIC PAINT THAT COORDINATE WITH YOUR PRINT— ONE DARK, ONE LIGHT ◼ 2 SHEETS OF PAPER, EACH 8½ x 11 INCHES (21.6 x 27.9 CM) ◼ TAPE ◼ 2 STENCIL BLANKS, EACH 8½ x 11 INCHES (21.6 x 27.9 CM) ◼ SPRAY STENCIL ADHESIVE ◼ TWO ¾-INCH (1.9 CM) OR 1-INCH (2.5 CM) STENCIL BRUSHES ◼ ROTARY CUTTER (OPTIONAL)

WHAT YOU DO

1 Sand the media tower to prepare it for painting. Wipe any dust away with a tack cloth or a damp paper towel.

2 Paint the entire media tower with the white paint Ⓐ. Apply several coats, allowing each coat to dry before applying the next one.

3 Prepare the fabric with Fabric Mod Podge Ⓑ (page 12). Allow to dry.

4 While the fabric is drying, paint the inside back of the tower with the darker paint. (For this project I used dark purple.) Apply at least two coats, allowing each coat to dry before applying the next one.

5 Create two stencils following the instructions in Making A Stencil on page 59. Working with one stencil at a time, use the spray stencil adhesive to attach the stencil to the back of the shelf (don't forget to include the small parts). Place masking tape around the edges, if desired, to further secure the stencil.

MODERN CHAIRS MEDIA TOWER

MAKING A STENCIL

You can use purchased stencil blanks to make your stencils, or try using freezer paper you can buy at the grocery store.

1. Choose the motif you want to stencil. For this project, I selected two chairs to coordinate with my fabric.

2. Use a pencil to draw your motif on two separate sheets of paper. Make sure it will fit between the shelves of the tower. You can draw the motifs by hand, or find clip art on the web.

3. Tape a stencil blank to the top of each piece of paper, and place them on the self-healing mat. Use a craft knife to cut out each stencil. Do not discard the small parts as you'll need them to complete the design.

6   Stencil the design using the lighter color Ⓒ (I used fuchsia) and a stencil brush. Remove the stencil immediately after painting (use tweezers to help peel it away if necessary), and allow to dry. Repeat for each shelf.

7   Carefully measure both sides of the tower, and cut the fabric to fit. Use a rotary cutter if you have one.

8   Use the Fabric Mod Podge to glue the fabric to both sides of the tower. Smooth the fabric carefully with your hands and use the brayer to remove any bubbles. Allow to dry for 15 to 20 minutes. Trim any excess fabric with a craft knife, if necessary.

9   Use the Hard Coat Mod Podge to seal the entire tower Ⓓ. Allow to dry. Apply at least two more coats, allowing the Mod Podge to dry between each one. Let dry for 24 hours before using.

JEWEL TONE WRAPPING-PAPER STOOL

I don't know about you, but I always have a surplus of wrapping paper around. I've either already wrapped a gift, or the paper is too pretty and I can't bear to throw it away. So here's a great solution: incorporate the paper into your home décor. This paper had such a nice pattern that I felt it had a different destination than the trash bin after the birthday party. Now I think it's right where it belongs!

WHAT YOU'LL NEED MOD PODGE TOOL KIT (PAGE 13) ▪ HARD COAT MOD PODGE ▪ UNFINISHED WOODEN STOOL ▪ TACK CLOTH OR PAPER TOWELS ▪ WRAPPING PAPER IN A PATTERN OF CHOICE ▪ ACRYLIC CRAFT PAINT IN KHAKI, INK BLUE, AND DARK TURQUOISE ▪ SPRAY BOTTLE (OPTIONAL)

WHAT YOU DO

1 Sand the surface to prepare it for painting. Use a tack cloth or damp paper towel to wipe away any dust.

2 Carefully measure both steps on your stool, and cut the wrapping paper to fit Ⓐ. Set aside.

3 Paint the tops of the steps using the khaki paint. Use the ink blue to paint the edges of the steps, and the dark turquoise to paint the remaining frame Ⓑ. Allow to dry.

4 Apply a medium layer of the Hard Coat Mod Podge to the top of one step. Use your hands to smooth the paper down and a brayer for further smoothing Ⓒ. Keep smoothing until all bubbles are gone. Repeat on the second step. Allow to dry for 15 to 20 minutes.

5 On the step with the cutout, use the craft knife to carefully cut the paper away from the hole, and discard.

JEWEL TONE WRAPPING-PAPER STOOL

6 Coat the entire stool with two coats of Mod Podge Ⓓ, allowing the first coat to dry before applying the second. Allow to dry for 24 hours before using.

TIP → *If you're working with a thin wrapping paper, it's a good idea to spray it with a light mist of water before Mod Podging to prevent wrinkles.*

I need a message center because I can't keep everything straight. I think this is true for most people today, and especially for all creative types. I've been known to look for my phone while I'm talking on it! I wanted a message board that was truly unique; something that could keep notes but still looked pretty. Using chalkboard paint to make this board was a perfect solution. If you'd rather pin your notes, you can always glue cork to some of the tiles.

WHAT YOU'LL NEED   MOD PODGE TOOL KIT (PAGE 13)   ■   MATTE MOD PODGE   ■   WOODEN PUZZLE BOARD WITH NINE TILES   ■   ACRYLIC PAINT IN BLACK AND MUSTARD YELLOW   ■   BLACK CHALKBOARD PAINT   ■ 3 SHEETS OF DOUBLE-SIDED SCRAPBOOK PAPER   ■   SMALL BROWN RAFFLE TICKETS   ■   RAFFLE TICKET STAMP AND INK PAD   ■   SPRAY FIXATIVE (OPTIONAL)   ■   EMBELLISHMENTS, INCLUDING KEYS, ALPHABET TAPE, SELF-ADHESIVE RHINESTONES   ■   SEVERAL BLACK BUTTONS IN VARIOUS SIZES   ■   PAPER DOILY   ■   CHALK

WHAT YOU DO

1   Remove the wooden tiles from the frame, then paint the entire frame with the black acrylic paint. Allow to dry. Paint five of the wooden tiles mustard yellow, and allow to dry.

2   Paint the remaining four tiles with chalkboard paint Ⓐ. Use a foam brush for best results and apply at least three coats, allowing each coat to dry between applications. Set these aside to keep them separate from the tiles you painted with the mustard yellow paint.

3   Select the scrapbook papers you want to use. Lay the five tiles painted mustard yellow on the back of the papers, trace around them, and then cut them out.

4   Apply a medium layer of Mod Podge to the surface of one black tile. Place one of the cut papers on the surface and smooth thoroughly with your hands or a brayer. Repeat for the other four tiles. Allow to dry for 15 to 20 minutes

5   While the five tiles are drying, paint the doily mustard yellow and allow to dry.

6   Create a few raffle tickets with the raffle stamp and let them dry.

   DESIGNER NOTE → *Test your ink to see if it smears. If it does, use spray fixative to seal the ink before Mod Podging.*

7   Go back and use the Mod Podge to seal the five tiles you covered with paper Ⓑ. Mod Podge the entire frame with two coats, allowing the first coat to dry before applying the second. Allow to dry.

8   Create the dotted pattern on the edge of the frame using a large button as your template. Measure to determine the placement, and then lay the button on the frame. With a pencil, lightly draw around the curve of the button. Use the mustard yellow paint and a small brush to dot the paint around the line Ⓒ. Allow to dry.

9   Now it's time to embellish the five mustard yellow tiles. I Mod Podged the tickets and doily Ⓓ. Then I used craft glue to apply the rhinestones, buttons, and alphabet tape, and finally black embroidery thread to attach the keys and tape to secure them.

10   To finish, use craft glue to adhere all the tiles to the board and allow to dry. Use the chalk to prepare the chalkboard paint for use following the manufacturer's instructions.

MODERN FOREST TOY BOX

·TOYS·

I really enjoyed giving this toy chest a new life, but it wasn't without its struggles. My number one piece of advice for covering a large, flat surface is to measure very carefully and cut slowly so that your fabric matches exactly. My second piece of advice is to work in sections since the Mod Podge dries quickly. Follow these, and you'll be a Podging success story with bragging rights over a toy chest!

WHAT YOU'LL NEED MOD PODGE TOOL KIT (PAGE 13) FABRIC MOD PODGE HARD COAT MOD PODGE OLD TOY CHEST TACK CLOTH OR PAPER TOWELS 3 YARDS (2.7 M) OF FABRIC, OR ENOUGH TO COVER THE CHEST ACRYLIC PAINT IN WHITE (OPTIONAL), PINK, YELLOW-GREEN, MAGENTA, AND DARK BROWN 1 STENCIL SHEET, AT LEAST 4 x 6 INCHES (10.2 x 15.2 CM) STENCIL TAPE STENCIL BRUSH ½-INCH (1.3 CM) PAINT DAUBER

WHAT YOU DO

1 Use whatever tools needed to disassemble the toy chest and set the hardware aside. Prepare the surface by sanding, then use a tack cloth or paper towel to wipe away any dust.

   TIP → *You may not need to disassemble your toy chest. If you can easily maneuver the chest for tracing the pieces onto the fabric in step 2, you can leave it in one piece.*

2 Lay the lid of the toy chest on the back of the fabric, and trace around it. This will give you an idea of how large an area you'll need to Mod Podge. Repeat for the sides of the chest.

3 Prepare the fabric with Fabric Mod Podge Ⓐ (page 12). Allow to dry, then cut out the fabric pieces and set aside.

4 Reassemble the chest.

5 Paint the toy chest in the colors you desire Ⓑ.

DESIGNER NOTE → *I painted the lid, back, and sides of the chest with dark brown. I painted the front with pink, magenta, and yellow-green. Apply several coats, allowing each coat to dry before applying the next one.*

DESIGNER NOTE → *If you're using light-colored fabric, you may want to apply a base coat of white paint to the areas of the chest where you'll be Mod Podging the fabric. Doing so will prevent the darker surface color from dulling the fabric. Apply the paint, and allow to dry.*

6 Mod Podge the fabric to the toy chest Ⓒ. Work one piece at a time, from left to right. Keep Mod Podging and smoothing until you reach the edge of the lid. Allow to dry for 15 to 20 minutes. Repeat this step for the sides.

DESIGNER NOTE → *I worked the lid in four sections, applying the Mod Podge and smoothing the fabric as I went.*

7 While the Mod Podge is drying, make a stencil for the word TOYS.

DESIGNER NOTE → *I used a text program on my computer to create the word in a font that I liked, making it bold and large. I traced the word on the stencil sheet and cut each letter out individually (see Making A Stencil on page 59).*

8 Use the stencil tape to attach the stencil to the toy chest. Stencil the word with a coordinating acrylic paint color and the stencil brush. Remove the stencil immediately after painting, and allow to dry.

9 Use the paint dauber to add dots of contrasting paint to each side of your word. Allow to dry.

10 Apply a coat of the Hard Coat Mod Podge to the entire chest Ⓓ. Allow to dry. Apply at least two more coats, allowing each coat to dry before applying the next one. Allow to dry 24 hours before using.

MAGIC WASHI TAPE CLOCK

Jen is one of the first friends I made online, and one of the first people I featured on my website. I will never tell her this in person, but she's a much better Mod Podger than I am. Jen did a great job using washi tape and Dimensional Magic on this clock. It's worthy of hanging on my wall, and very pretty, like all of her projects.

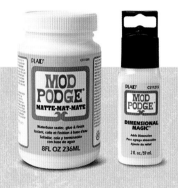

WHAT YOU'LL NEED MOD PODGE TOOL KIT (PAGE 13) ▪ MATTE MOD PODGE ▪ DIMENSIONAL MAGIC MOD PODGE ▪ INEXPENSIVE CLOCK ▪ 1 SHEET OF SCRAPBOOK PAPER ▪ WAX PAPER ▪ REPURPOSED SCRABBLE® TILES ▪ WASHI TAPE IN A VARIETY OF PATTERNS ▪ HOT GLUE AND GLUE STICKS

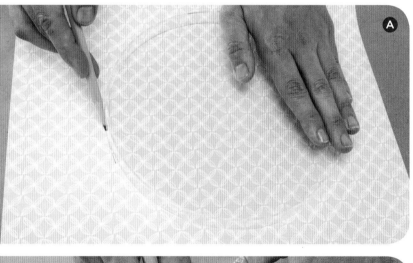

WHAT YOU DO

1 Start with an inexpensive clock, and remove the clear cover. Take off the hands, and set aside.

2 If your clock has a paper face that you can remove, take it off and use it to trace around on the scrapbook paper and wax paper Ⓐ. If you can't remove the paper, trace around the clear cover. Cut out the face from the scrapbook paper and wax paper.

3 Lay the wax paper over the clock face. Use a pencil to mark the position of the numbers. Poke the pencil through the wax paper at the center of the face to mark the hole for the hands Ⓑ.

4 Transfer the marks onto the cutout paper face. Apply a medium layer of the Matte Mod Podge to the clock face. Position the paper over it, and use your fingers to smooth it down. Allow to dry for 15 to 20 minutes.

5   Apply two topcoats of Mod Podge to the paper Ⓒ. Allow the first coat to dry before applying the second. Allow to dry.

6   Trace the tiles on the various washi tapes. Cut them out and then stick the tape to the tiles. Apply the Dimensional Magic Mod Podge over the top of the tiles Ⓓ, and allow to dry.

7   Use hot glue to attach the tiles to the clock face.

8   Replace the hands of the clock.

   DESIGNER NOTE → *The plastic hands on my clock were too long to get over the tiles so I trimmed them with nail clippers. If you have a similar problem with metal hands, use wire snips to trim them.*

   TIP → *For the tiles, buy an old Scrabble game at a thrift store. They're perfect for this project, and you can use the leftovers in a hundred different ways for other crafty endeavors. You can also find lots of great tiles on Etsy.*

Combine a practical item with a bit of Mod Podge, and you have something worthy of the kitchen table. I love Jenny's whimsical and artistic style, and I also love the way she sews paper to use in her projects. The sentiment she added to the top gives this Lazy Susan that much more charm. Happy spinning!

WHAT YOU'LL NEED MOD PODGE TOOL KIT (PAGE 13) ◼ GLOSS OR MATTE MOD PODGE ◼ BROWN PAPER BAG ◼ SEWING MACHINE ◼ DARNING FOOT ◼ THREAD ◼ WOODEN LAZY SUSAN ◼ WHITE GESSO ◼ ASSORTED PAPER SCRAPS ◼ CIRCLE PUNCHES IN VARIOUS SIZES ◼ GRAPHITE PENCIL ◼ SPRAY FIXATIVE ◼ ACRYLIC PAINTS

WHAT YOU DO

1 Cut out a heart shape from the brown paper bag.

2 Free motion stitch a selected text onto the cutout heart.

   DESIGNER NOTE → *In order to free motion stitch, lower the feed dogs on your sewing machine and attach a darning foot. An alternative to free motion stitching is to hand embroider the text.*

3 Apply two coats of white gesso to the wooden lazy Susan using a brush Ⓐ. Allow the gesso to dry in between coats.

4 Adhere the free motion stitched heart onto the center of the lazy Susan with the Gloss or Matte Mod Podge Ⓑ.

5 Use the punches to punch circles from the assorted papers (like vintage wallpaper, sheet music, or decorative paper bags). Mod Podge the circles to the perimeter of the lazy Susan.

6 With the graphite pencil, add shading to the adhered heart and circles Ⓒ. Apply with gentle strokes, and then use your fingers to smudge the lines. Add more details with the graphite pencil as desired.

7 After completing the shading and details, use the spray fixative to prevent the graphite from smudging further.

8 Paint dots of acrylic paint with the point of a pencil or the end of a paintbrush to add detail.

9 Apply two coats of Mod Podge to the entire lazy Susan. Allow the first coat to dry before applying the second. Wait 24 hours before using.

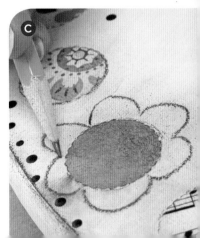

SEWING NOTIONS RIBBON ORGANIZER

I have so many small spools of ribbon sitting at the bottom of a drawer. This means that a lot of nice ribbon isn't getting used because I can't see it. The real problem is that the smaller ribbons don't fit in the ribbon organizers found in stores—and I have a lot of those types of ribbon. So what does a crafter do? She doesn't complain. She simply creates a solution.

WHAT YOU'LL NEED   MOD PODGE TOOL KIT (PAGE 13)   ▪   MATTE MOD PODGE   ▪
DIMENSIONAL MAGIC MOD PODGE   ▪   RECTANGULAR PAPIER-MÂCHÉ BOX   ▪   SMALL SAW   ▪
TWO ½-INCH (1.3 CM) DOWELS, EACH AT LEAST 12 INCHES (30.5 CM) LONG   ▪   ACRYLIC PAINT
IN PINK, GREEN, BLUE, SILVER, WHITE, BLACK, YELLOW, MAGENTA   ▪   HAND DRILL   ▪   CHIPBOARD
SCRAPBOOK EMBELLISHMENTS, SUCH AS SCISSORS, DRESS FORM, AND SEWING MACHINE   ▪
2 SHEETS OF COORDINATING SCRAPBOOK PAPER   ▪   OVAL STENCIL OR TEMPLATE   ▪
2 FEET (61 CM) OF MEASURING-TAPE RIBBON

WHAT YOU DO

1   Measure a long side of the papier-mâché box. Use the small saw to cut the dowels approximately ⅛ inch (3 mm) longer than this measurement. Sand the ends of the dowels to smooth them, then paint the dowels pink. Allow to dry, and set aside.

2   Determine the position of the dowels in the box. Make sure two rolls of ribbon will fit across the width of the box. Measure carefully, and drill with the hand drill.
DESIGNER NOTE →   *This box was 9 inches (22.9 cm) long. Each hole was 3 inches (7.6 cm) up from the bottom and 1 inch (2.5 cm) in from the sides.*

3   Sand the box where you drilled to remove any excess paper from around the holes.

4   Paint the bottom of the box blue and the lid green. Apply several coats, allowing each to dry before brushing on the next one.

5   Paint the chipboard scrapbook embellishments.
DESIGNER NOTE →   *I used leftover paint colors and painted the designs on the shapes freehand.*

6   Cut 1-inch-wide (2.5 cm) paper strips to fit the side of the box from a sheet of scrapbook paper. Set aside.

7   Use the oval stencil or template to cut an oval from the coordinating piece of paper.

8   Apply a medium layer of the Matte Mod Podge to glue the oval to the top of the box. Do the same to glue the strips to the side of the box Ⓐ. Allow to dry for 15 to 20 minutes.

9   Once dry, Mod Podge the entire box and lid, inside and out, to seal. Apply several coats, allowing each one to dry before applying the next one.

SEWING NOTIONS RIBBON ORGANIZER

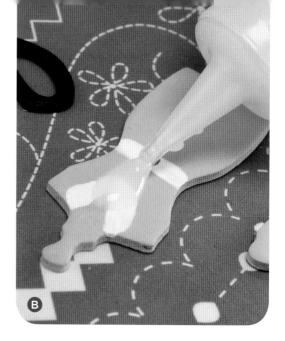

10 Use craft glue to glue the measuring-tape ribbon around the edges of the lid. Glue the painted chipboard shapes to the oval. Allow to dry.

11 Apply the Dimensional Magic Mod Podge to the top of the chipboard pieces on the oval Ⓑ, and allow to dry.

12 Insert the painted dowels, and you're ready to get organized!

TIP → *If your ribbon doesn't have holes in the center of the spool (mine didn't), then use the hand drill to make a hole large enough for your dowel rod to fit through it.*

**SUPER GIRLY
WALL CUBES**

If you're looking for an alternative to plain shelving, these may be more interesting than simple white boards. I spotted these cube shelves at one of my favorite stores and realized the deep sides were perfect for Mod Podging. I took the opportunity to use girly paper for these so that you could see what they would look like in a child's room. However, you can certainly make them more adult and hang them anywhere in your house.

WHAT YOU'LL NEED   MOD PODGE TOOL KIT (PAGE 13) ■ MATTE MOD PODGE ■ 3 WHITE WOODEN CUBE SHELVES, ONE EACH IN SMALL, MEDIUM, AND LARGE ■ 2 SHEETS OF SCRAPBOOK PAPER IN COORDINATING PATTERNS ■ 3 COORDINATING PAPER RIBBONS ■ HOT GLUE AND GLUE STICKS ■ PAPER FLOWERS ■ BUTTONS

WHAT YOU DO

1 Starting with the largest shelf, measure the length and width of one side. Cut a piece of scrapbook paper to fit the length exactly, but cut the width approximately ½ inch (1.3 cm) less than your measurement. Make three more pieces just like this one. You'll need four pieces for each cube.

2 Repeat step 1 for the medium and small shelves.

3 Choose which paper ribbon you'll use for each shelf, and cut lengths to fit all four sides of each shelf. Set the ribbons aside.

4 Beginning with the largest shelf, apply a medium layer of Matte Mod Podge to one side, and glue a piece of scrapbook paper to it. Center the paper on the width, leaving ¼ inch (6 mm) of the paint showing on either side. Smooth with your fingers, and use a brayer to remove any air bubbles Ⓐ. Allow to dry for 15 to 20 minutes. Repeat on the remaining three sides.

5 Repeat step 4 on the medium and small shelves. Allow to dry, then Mod Podge all three shelves with a medium layer of Mod Podge on all four sides Ⓑ. Allow to dry.

Ⓐ

6 Apply a medium layer of Mod Podge down
the center of one side of a shelf. Lay the
ribbon over it, hold in place for a few
seconds, and then Mod Podge over the
top for a finish coat. Use a paintbrush to
wipe away any excess Mod Podge. Glue
ribbon on the remaining three sides. Repeat
on all three shelves, and allow to dry.

7 Use hot glue to randomly attach the
paper flowers and buttons to the front of
each shelf ⓒ. Allow to dry 24 hours
before using. Hang the shelves with the
hardware provided.

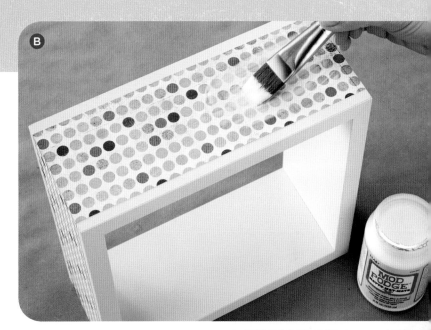

CHI-CHI MAGAZINE HOLDERS

Are you like me? I have magazine subscriptions to nearly every craft and home décor publication on the planet, and I never throw them away. Before the stacks take over your house, and the fire department gets involved, organize your collection by making crafty, customized magazine holders. Like everything, I believe even organizing should be as pretty as possible.

WHAT YOU'LL NEED   MOD PODGE TOOL KIT (PAGE 13)   ■   SATIN MOD PODGE   ■   MAGAZINE HOLDERS   ■   2 LARGE SHEETS OF DECORATIVE PAPER, EACH AT LEAST 20 x 30 INCHES (50.8 x 76.2 CM)   ■   ACRYLIC PAINT IN WHITE, HOT PINK, AND GOLD   ■   SPRAY WATER BOTTLE (OPTIONAL)

WHAT YOU DO

1   Trace each side of your magazine holders onto the backs of both sheets of paper. Cut them out and set them aside.

2   Use the white paint to apply a base coat to the magazine holders Ⓐ. Paint the edges to coordinate with the paper you're using. Apply several coats of paint, allowing each coat to dry before applying the next one. Allow to dry.

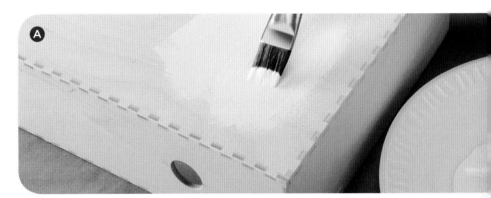

3   Use the Satin Mod Podge to glue the paper to both sides of each holder. Smooth out any air bubbles with the brayer Ⓑ. Allow to dry for 15 to 20 minutes.

4   Apply two topcoats to each holder. Let the first coat dry before applying the second. Allow to dry for 24 hours before using.

TIP →   *When using thinner paper, it helps to spray it with water before Mod Podging to prevent wrinkles Ⓒ. If needed, use the spray water bottle to spritz the paper, and then immediately Mod Podge it to the side of the magazine holder. To avoid tearing the paper, use the brayer to carefully roll out the wrinkles.*

RETRO FLORAL OUTDOOR CHAIR

I'm a huge fan of retro outdoor furniture, and have found more than one at my local thrift stores that I'd like to make over. With a little spray paint and fabric you can add just enough of a contemporary feel to bridge the decades. Then, when you're done, you can sit in it and have family members fan you and feed you grapes to reward you for all your hard work!

WHAT YOU'LL NEED   MOD PODGE TOOL KIT (PAGE 13)   ■   FABRIC MOD PODGE   ■   OUTDOOR MOD PODGE   ■   METAL OUTDOOR CHAIR   ■   #0000 STEEL WOOL   ■   SPRAY PAINT, SUITABLE FOR OUTDOOR METAL   ■   FABRIC   ■   CLEAR ACRYLIC ENAMEL OUTDOOR SEALER (OPTIONAL)

WHAT YOU DO

1   Some chairs will require more preparation than others. At the very least you'll need to sand the chair using the #0000 steel wool over the entire surface to remove old paint flecks and rust. Then spray the chair with paint formulated for metal that will live outdoors. After prepping, allow the chair to dry for at least 24 hours before Mod Podging.

2   Prepare fabric with Fabric Mod Podge (page 12) Ⓐ. Allow to dry.

3   Carefully measure both the seat and the back of the chair. Cut the fabric to fit using scissors Ⓑ.

4   Begin with the seat. Working left to right, apply a medium layer of the Outdoor Mod Podge to a small area Ⓒ, and then smooth the fabric down onto the seat. Continue applying the Mod Podge one area at a time and smoothing down the fabric as you go. Allow to dry for 15 to 20 minutes. Use a paintbrush to wipe away any excess Mod Podge.

5   Repeat step 4 on the back of the chair. Apply two coats of Mod Podge to seal, allowing the first coat to dry before applying the second.

6   To protect your chair for years to come, I highly recommend that you seal the chair with a layer of clear acrylic enamel outdoor sealer.

HARLEQUIN CRAFT SUPPLY ORGANIZERS

DESIGNER: *Julie Lewis*

I have enough supplies to keep a small country crafting for at least six months. One thing I'm always in need of is ways to organize my goodies, especially deeper containers that will hold things like brushes, dowel rods, and markers. These containers make a great addition to any desktop, and you can always find inexpensive ceramic pots at your favorite craft stores.

WHAT YOU'LL NEED   MOD PODGE TOOL KIT (PAGE 13) ■ SATIN MOD PODGE ■ 2 CERAMIC POTS ■
VELLUM ■ 2 SHEETS OF SCRAPBOOK PAPER ■ 2 SMALL ROLLS OF COORDINATING RIBBON ■
6 FELT BUTTONS ■ 6 WOODEN BUTTONS

WHAT YOU DO

1 Measure the circumference of each container. Divide that number by the number of diamonds you want to go around the middle.

DESIGNER NOTE → *For example, my container measured 14 inches (35.6 cm). I estimated that I would need seven diamonds, each approximately 2 inches (5 cm) wide.*

2 Add ¼ inch (6 mm) to that measurement to accommodate an overlap.

DESIGNER NOTE → *With the addition, my diamonds measured 2¼ inches (5.7 cm) wide.*

3 Measure the height of the pot, and then subtract 1 inch (2.5 cm).

DESIGNER NOTE → *My pot measured 7 inches (17.8 cm); I subtracted an inch to come up with 6 inches (15.2 cm).*

4 Use the vellum to make a diamond template based on your measurements. Once you have a template, cut seven diamonds out of one sheet of scrapbook paper for one pot, and the same amount from the second sheet for the other pot.

5 Apply a medium layer of Satin Mod Podge to one of your pots, and smooth a cut diamond over it. Use a brush to wipe away any excess Mod Podge. Repeat, using the remaining six diamonds, overlapping them slightly as you work around the pot.

6 Repeat for the second pot, and allow each pot to dry for 15 to 20 minutes.

7 Seal both pots with at least two coats of Mod Podge Ⓐ. Allow the first coat to dry before applying the second.

8 Measure the distance diagonally from the top of the pot at the center between diamonds to the bottom of the pot at the center between diamonds. Cut 14 strips of ribbon from each color (14 strips for each pot) to their respective measurements.

9 Use craft glue to adhere the ribbon to the pots Ⓑ. Glue the buttons at the point where the diamonds overlap. Allow to dry for 24 hours before using.

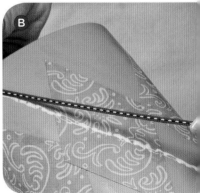

BE A DEER SUITCASE

I fondly remember my parents' brown luggage that we used for traveling during the 1980s. I also fondly remember that it weighed as much as a small child. Thank goodness suitcases have gotten lighter! The funny thing is that refurbishing luggage has become popular, but not necessarily for travel. People are fixing up suitcases for storage, room decorations, and even for cool craft-fair displays. Since silhouettes are never going to go out of style, I added one on the front for interest.

WHAT YOU'LL NEED MOD PODGE TOOL KIT (PAGE 13) ■ FABRIC MOD PODGE ■ SATIN MOD PODGE ■ OLD SUITCASE ■ OUTDOOR PAINT IN AQUA AND WHITE ■ 2 YARDS (1.8 M) OF FABRIC ■ CLIP-ART SILHOUETTE ■ STENCIL TAPE ■ ¼ YARD (22.9 CM) FABRIC IN A COORDINATING PRINT OR SOLID ■ CLEAR ACRYLIC SPRAY SEALER

WHAT YOU DO

1 Prepare the fabric with the Fabric Mod Podge (page 12), and allow to dry Ⓐ.

2 Paint both sides of the main body of the suitcase using the white outdoor paint. Do the trim using the aqua paint. Apply several coats, allowing each to dry before applying the next.

DESIGNER NOTE → *Painting the suitcase with a white base coat prevents the original color from dulling the fabric color.*

DESIGNER NOTE → *Rather than first making a pattern for cutting the fabric, I used Mod Podge to adhere larger pieces of the prepared fabric directly to the suitcase. Then I used a sharp craft knife to trim the fabric to fit. However, if you desire, you could make a pattern for cutting the fabric.*

3 Work on a small area of each section of the suitcase at a time. Apply a medium layer of Mod Podge to a section of the suitcase, and lay a piece of the fabric on it. Smooth the fabric toward the edges of the section, but do not glue the edges down.

4 Use a sharp craft knife to trim the fabric to fit Ⓑ before finally Mod Podging the fabric to the edges of each section.

5 Print a clip-art silhouette of choice from the Internet using royalty-free clip art, and then cut it out with the craft knife Ⓒ.

6 Use the stencil tape to adhere the silhouette to the contrasting fabric, and then use scissors to cut it out.

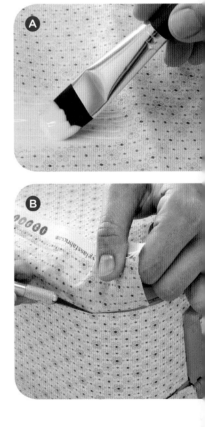

7 Apply a medium layer of Mod Podge onto the surface of the suitcase where you want the silhouette to go. Lay the silhouette on the Mod Podge, and smooth carefully. Allow to dry for 15 to 20 minutes.

8 Paint at least two coats of the Satin Mod Podge over the entire surface of the suitcase, including the silhouette and trim Ⓓ. Be careful to avoid brushing the hardware.

9 Allow to dry for 24 hours before using. I highly recommend spraying the entire suitcase with the clear acrylic sealer to reduce any tackiness and to add durability.

TIP → *Take your time and work slowly on this project when applying and cutting the fabric to fit. Doing so will result in clean edges. Trim carefully, especially around the hardware.*

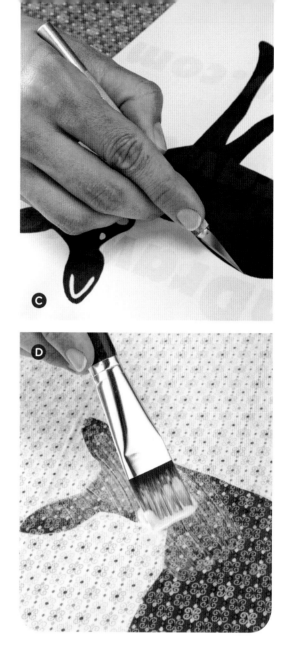

Ⓒ

Ⓓ

HAPPY MUSHROOM OUTDOOR PLANTER

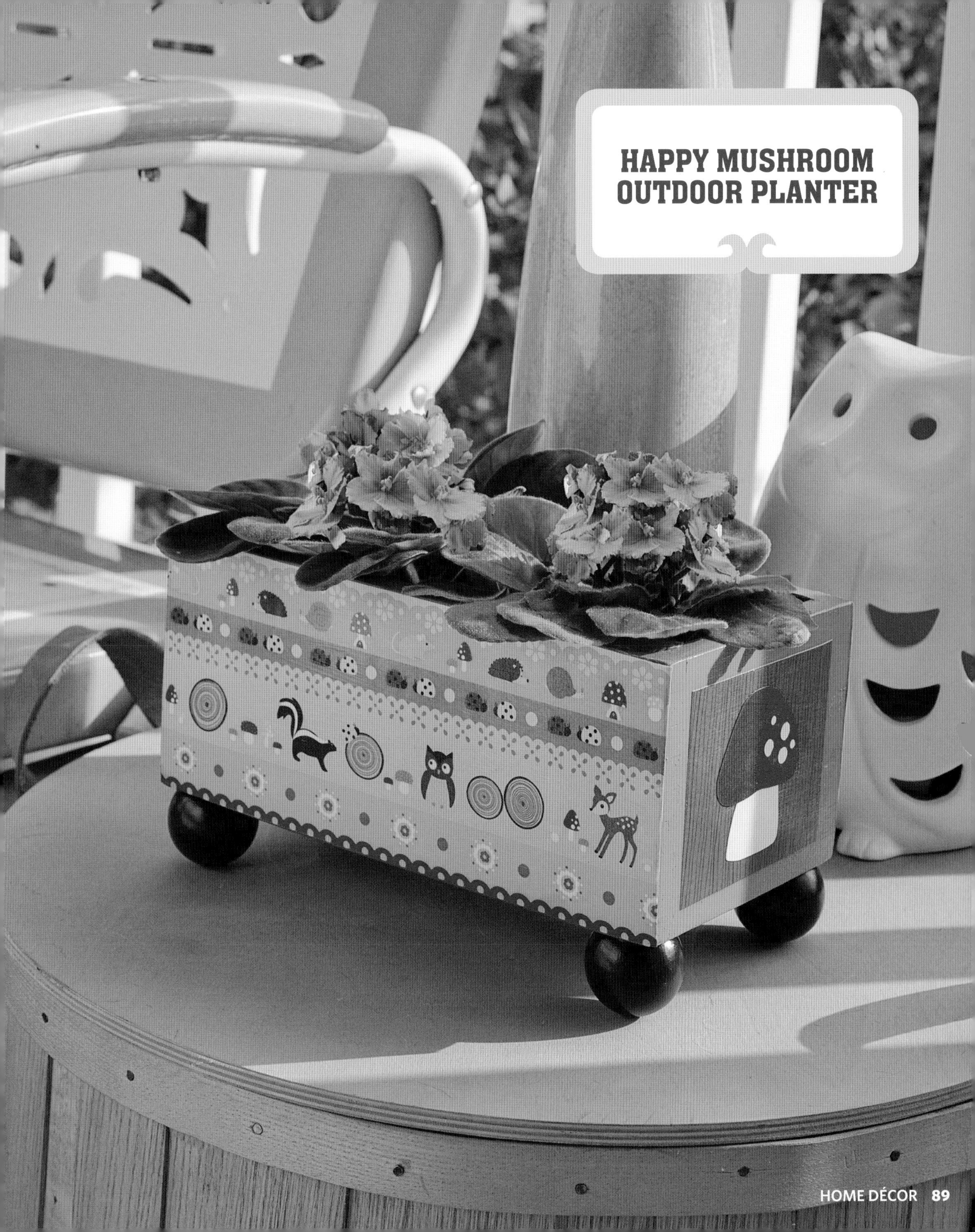

HAPPY MUSHROOM OUTDOOR PLANTER

If I could cover every outdoor item I own with forest-themed scrapbook paper, I definitely would. There's something about the mushrooms and deer that makes plants look more at home. I guess my philosophy is why have plain planters when you don't have to?

WHAT YOU'LL NEED MOD PODGE TOOL KIT (PAGE 13) ■ OUTDOOR MOD PODGE ■ RECTANGULAR WOODEN PLANTER WITH TRAY ■ OUTDOOR ACRYLIC PAINT IN GREEN, ORANGE, AND DARK BROWN ■ 4 WOODEN BALL FEET, 1 INCH (2.5 CM) IN DIAMETER ■ 2 SHEETS OF OUTDOOR-THEMED SCRAPBOOK PAPER ■ CARDSTOCK IN RED AND CREAM ■ $1/16$-INCH (1.6 MM) AND $1/4$-INCH (6 MM) HOLE PUNCHES

WHAT YOU DO

1 Remove the planter from the tray while working. Use the outdoor acrylic paint to paint the planter green on the outside and orange on the inside Ⓐ. Paint the ball feet dark brown and the tray green.

2 Carefully measure the planter, and cut the scrapbook paper to fit Ⓑ. For the long sides, cut the paper to fit exactly. For the ends, leave a $1/2$-inch (1.3 cm) seam allowance around the edge to show off the color of the container. Set the paper aside.

3 Hand draw a mushroom shape, and then cut it apart to separate the cap from the stem. Trace two caps on the red cardstock, and cut out. Trace two stems on the cream cardstock, and cut out. Use the hole punches to create an assortment of cream spots to go on the red caps. Set aside.

4 Starting with a long side of the planter, apply a medium layer of the Outdoor Mod Podge Ⓒ. Carefully align the paper to the side of the planter. Use your fingers to smooth the paper, and a brayer if necessary to remove any bubbles. Trim away any excess paper with a craft knife. Repeat for the other side. Allow to dry for 15 to 20 minutes.

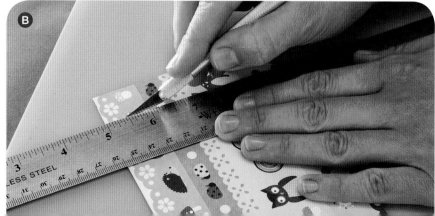

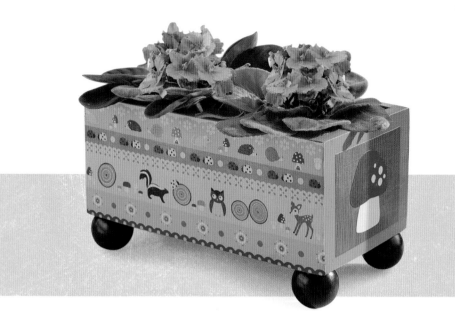

5   Coat both sides of the paper with a single layer of Outdoor Mod Podge as a finish coat, and allow to dry Ⓓ.

6   On one of the ends, apply a medium layer of Outdoor Mod Podge and place the paper, smoothing it with your fingers, and using a brayer or squeegee if necessary. Repeat on the other end and allow to dry for 15 to 20 minutes.

7   Mod Podge a mushroom on each of the ends (don't forget the spots!). Allow to dry. Cover the ends with a layer of Mod Podge as a finish coat and allow to dry.

8   Apply two coats of Outdoor Mod Podge to the entire container, the four ball feet, and the tray. Let the first coat dry before applying the second. Allow to dry.

9   Use craft glue to attach the ball feet. Allow to dry for 24 hours. Insert the tray into the planter before using.

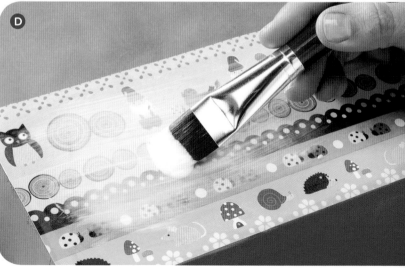

ACEY-DEUCEY BACKGAMMON

DESIGNER: **Beckie Farrant**

I was first drawn to this game redo by Beckie because of the bright colors—even though I had no idea what Acey-Deucey Backgammon was. But the way she gussied it up made me want to learn to play! This is a perfect example of why Beckie is amazing at her personal brand of turning trash into treasure.

WHAT YOU'LL NEED MOD PODGE TOOL KIT (PAGE 13)   ▢   GLOSS MOD PODGE   ▢   2 WOODEN TRAYS   ▢
HAMMER   ▢   WOOD FILLER (OPTIONAL)   ▢   SPRAY PRIMER   ▢   SPRAY PAINT   ▢   2 SHEETS OF DOUBLE-SIDED
SCRAPBOOK PAPER OR CARDSTOCK   ▢   ELECTRIC DRILL   ▢   2 SMALL HINGES   ▢   1 SMALL CLASP   ▢   DICE   ▢
30 GAME PIECES IN TWO COLORS, 15 OF EACH COLOR   ▢   SMALL BAG FOR STORING GAME PIECES

WHAT YOU DO

1 Use the hammer to remove any dividers that may be in the wooden trays. Use the wood filler to fill in any divots or holes in the wood.

DESIGNER NOTE → I prefer not to fill in the holes. I like the fact that you know it was something else in the past. I think it adds character to the finished piece.

2 Lightly sand the entire surface with 120-grit sandpaper. Use the spray primer to prime the trays, and then paint them with the spray paint.

3 Figure out the measurements for six triangles by first measuring the width of your tray. Divide that number by six. This number will be the base (width) of the triangle.

DESIGNER NOTE → For example, my tray measured 8½ inches (21.6 cm). When I divided by six, I got 1⅜ inches (3.5 cm). The height of my triangle was 4 inches (10.2 cm).

4 Use a craft knife with a self-healing mat or paper cutter to cut the triangles from one of the sheets of double-sided scrapbook paper or cardstock.

5 With a brush, apply an even coat of Mod Podge to the tray Ⓐ. Glue the triangles to the tray, alternating colors. Smooth with your hands to remove any bubbles.

6 Cut out the letters from the other sheet of scrapbook paper or cardstock to spell Acey Deucey.

DESIGNER NOTE → I used my computerized electronic cutting tool. You can also purchase scrapbook stickers to achieve the same effect.

7 Cover the backs of the letters with Mod Podge, and place them on the tray. When dry, apply two coats to the entire tray to seal Ⓑ. Make sure you allow the first coat to dry before applying the second.

8 Position the hinges, then mark the holes 1 inch (2.5 cm) from the edge of the tray. Use the electric drill to screw the hinges in place.

9 Position the clasp and screw it in place using the electric drill.

DESIGNER NOTE → I already had the dice and a small organza bag in my stash. I purchased two bags of small glass round beads (one clear, one turquoise) for the game pieces.

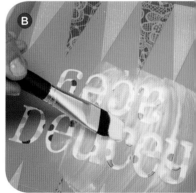

SPARKLE PAPER FLOWER WREATH

DESIGNER: *Julie Lewis*

Real flowers are beautiful, but there's something to be said for paper flowers that last year-round. This project was made using paper from my stash. You might find you have most of the supplies already at hand without needing to run to the store. It feels great to use my stash, like I'm recycling, but not really. Either way, this wreath is bright and fun—with an added touch of sparkle on the flowers to give it a little extra interest.

WHAT YOU'LL NEED MOD PODGE TOOL KIT (PAGE 13) ☐ SPARKLE MOD PODGE ☐
MATTE OR SATIN MOD PODGE ☐ WOODEN LEAF EMBELLISHMENTS ☐ ACRYLIC PAINT
IN MEDIUM GREEN, LIGHT BLUE, PINK, ORANGE, LIME GREEN, HOT PINK, AND FUCHSIA ☐
WHITE PAPER FLOWERS CUT FROM PAINTABLE PAPER ☐ ASSORTMENT OF COORDINATING
SHEETS OF SCRAPBOOK PAPER ☐ ZIGZAG DECORATIVE-EDGE SCISSORS ☐ FOAM WREATH
FORM ☐ CRAFT FOAM SCRAPS ☐ SMALL HOLE PUNCH

WHAT YOU DO

1 Paint the wooden leaf embellishments medium green. Apply several coats, allowing each to dry before applying the next. Allow to dry, and set aside.

2 Paint the paper flowers in various colors with craft paint. Apply several coats, allowing each coat to dry before applying the next.

DESIGNER NOTE → *Using various sizes of flowers (large, medium, and small) will allow you to layer them when you attach them to the wreath for a dimensional effect.*

3 Cover the flowers with one coat of the Sparkle Mod Podge Ⓐ. Set aside, and allow to dry.

4 Cut strips from the assortment of scrapbook papers using the zigzag decorative-edge scissors. Make at least 40 strips (though you may need more or less depending on how wide you cut them and the size of your wreath form).

5 Add a medium layer of the Matte or Satin Mod Podge around one portion of the foam wreath form. Wrap a strip around it, hold for a few seconds until the strip adheres Ⓑ, and then move on to the next strip. Alternate strips cut from different papers to add more interest. Repeat until the entire wreath is covered. Allow to dry for 15 to 20 minutes.

6 Coat the wreath with two layers of the Matte or Satin Mod Podge, allowing the first to dry before applying the second.

DESIGNER NOTE → *If you really want your wreath to shine, use the Sparkle Mod Podge to coat the wreath.*

7 Adhere the painted wooden leaves and paper flowers to the wreath in a random fashion with craft glue.

8 Use the small hole punch to make flower centers from the scraps of craft foam. Glue them to the flowers. Allow the entire wreath to dry for 24 hours before hanging.

ANTIQUE KEY WALL ART

One of the most popular projects on my blog was key wall art—though the original piece was in much brighter colors. Since I realize that not all of you wear bright green shirts with bright green socks like I do, I recreated the piece in a different color palette to offer you an option and inspiration. I like the earth tones and the more muted black print paper just as much as the original.

WHAT YOU'LL NEED   MOD PODGE TOOL KIT (PAGE 13) ▪ MATTE MOD PODGE ▪ INEXPENSIVE FRAME WITH A CARDBOARD BACK ▪ ACRYLIC PAINT IN METALLIC COPPER, WHITE, GRAY-BLUE, LIGHT GREEN, BLUE-GREEN, AND RED-ORANGE ▪ WOODEN CRAFT KEYS ▪ 1 SHEET OF SCRAPBOOK PAPER

WHAT YOU DO

1 Remove the cardboard back from the frame, and set aside.

2 Paint the frame using the metallic copper paint Ⓐ. Apply several coats, and allow each one to dry before applying the next.

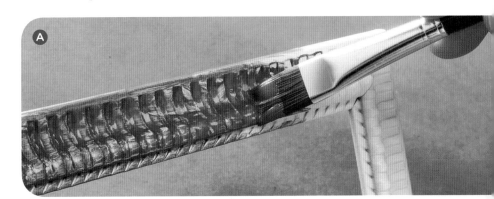

3 Use the remaining colors to carefully paint the wooden keys (they may be fragile), and allow to dry Ⓑ.

4 Trace the frame's cardboard back onto the sheet of scrapbook paper, and cut it out using a craft knife with self-sealing mat Ⓒ.

5 Apply a medium layer of the Matte Mod Podge to the cardboard back, and smooth the scrapbook paper down onto it. Allow to dry for 15 to 20 minutes.

6 Seal the papered cardboard with a layer of Mod Podge. Allow to dry.

7   Use craft glue to glue the keys to the paper on the cardboard back. Allow to dry, and then apply a sealing coat of Mod Podge Ⓓ. Let dry.

8   Attach the cardboard back to the frame using the craft glue. Allow to dry 24 hours before hanging.

HOLIDAY

Holidays are the most wonderful times of the year—the times when Mod Podge bottles make their way to craft tables all over the world. I use Mod Podge for handmade gifts, ornaments, decorations, party favors, and anything else you can think of. Whatever you are planning for your yearly celebrations, make Mod Podge an important part of the action with these great ideas.

MOD PODGE® ROCKS!

HALLOWEEN COUNTDOWN CALENDAR

A lot of people count the days to Christmas, but I count down to Halloween. After all, it's my favorite holiday to celebrate and to craft for. This calendar doesn't have to be just for kids. Try surprising your coworkers with one of these. It's all planned, really—you're totally buttering them up so they'll vote for you in the office costume competition!

WHAT YOU'LL NEED   MOD PODGE TOOL KIT (PAGE 13)   ■   GLOSS MOD PODGE   ■   ONE 24 x 30-INCH (61 x 76.2 CM) CANVAS   ■   ACRYLIC PAINT IN METALLIC WHITE, MEDIUM GRAY, BLACK, ORANGE, AND PLUM   ■   SILVER GLITTER PAINT   ■   30 PAPIER-MÂCHÉ BOXES, EACH 3 INCHES (7.6 CM) SQUARE   ■   1 PAPIER-MÂCHÉ BOX, 4 INCHES (10.2 CM) SQUARE   ■   ASSORTMENT OF HALLOWEEN-THEMED SCRAPBOOK PAPER, AT LEAST 12 SHEETS   ■   SCRAPBOOK PAPER IN LIGHT PURPLE, DARK PURPLE, ORANGE, AND BLACK   ■   DIE CUTTER OR TOOL TO MAKE NUMBERS 1 TO 31   ■   HALLOWEEN EMBELLISHMENTS, SUCH AS SPIDERS, CHIPBOARD SHAPES, AND BUTTONS   ■   HALLOWEEN CANDY AND PARTY FAVORS

WHAT YOU DO

1   Cover the canvas with several coats of the medium gray acrylic paint. Once the canvas is dry, apply several coats of the silver glitter paint, and allow to dry.

2   Trace each box lid onto a piece of scrapbook paper. Use random sheets of paper to add interest. Cut out, and set aside.

3   Paint all the papier-mâché boxes, using random colors of the acrylic paint for each one. Apply several coats, allowing each coat to dry before applying the next one.

4   While the boxes are drying, use your die cutter to cut the numbers 1 to 31 out of the solid-color papers. Cut out various sizes of numbers. You can even alter the fonts to make the project more fun!

5   Mod Podge the scrapbook papers to the lid of each box Ⓐ. Allow to dry, then apply a topcoat of Mod Podge to each box.

6 Mod Podge the numbers 1 to 30 randomly to the 3-inch (7.6 cm) box lids Ⓑ. Mod Podge the number 31 to the lid of the 4-inch (10.2 cm) box. Allow to dry. Use craft glue to attach an embellishment to each box

7 Use craft glue to glue the boxes to the canvas. Allow to dry for 24 hours before using. Place a small piece of Halloween candy or favor in each box, reserving the biggest and scariest for the 31st.

TIP → *If you don't have a die cutter, purchase stick-on numbers or use a number stencil to trace and cut your own from the solid-color scrapbook papers.*

GLOWING MUMMY HAND CANDY BOWL

DESIGNER: *Cathie Filian*

GLOWING MUMMY HAND CANDY BOWL

You could just dump the Halloween treats you're handing out into an old plastic storage container. Or, you could become the hit of the neighborhood with a decorated treat bowl complete with a ghoulishly glowing mummy hand. Designer Cathie Filian dares you to reach in and take two pieces.

WHAT YOU'LL NEED MOD PODGE TOOL KIT (PAGE 13) ▪ GLOSS MOD PODGE ▪ GLOW-IN-THE-DARK PAINT ▪ RUBBER KITCHEN GLOVE ▪ POLYESTER FIBERFILL ▪ CHOPSTICK OR KNITTING NEEDLE ▪ STAPLER ▪ 3 YARDS (2.7 M) OF CHEESECLOTH ▪ ACRYLIC PAINT IN REDDISH BROWN AND GRAY ▪ SEA SPONGE OR PAPER TOWEL ▪ GLASS BOWL ▪ 1 LARGE SHEET OF BLACK TISSUE PAPER ▪ SKULL-THEMED SCRAPBOOK PAPER OR FABRIC ▪ GATHERED-LACE TRIM, ENOUGH TO GO AROUND THE LIP OF THE BOWL ▪ VELVET RIBBON, ENOUGH TO GO AROUND THE LIP OF THE BOWL ▪ HOT GLUE GUN AND GLUE STICKS

WHAT YOU DO

1 Firmly stuff the glove with the polyester fiberfill Ⓐ. Use the chopstick or knitting needle to push the stuffing into the fingers of the glove. Staple the open ends of the glove to seal in the stuffing.

2 Cut 1 yard (.9 m) of the cheesecloth into long strips, each approximately 2 inches (5 cm) wide, and set aside.

3 Use the remaining two yards of cheesecloth to wrap the glove, starting at the stapled end. Apply a thick coat of the Gloss Mod Podge on the cheesecloth and glove as you go Ⓑ, Mod Podging until the fingers are almost all covered.

4 Saturate the cut strips of cheesecloth with Gloss Mod Podge. Use them for wrapping around the fingers and for filling in any gaps in the wrapping. Allow to dry 4 hours.

5 Dip a damp sea sponge or a damp crunched paper towel into the reddish brown and gray paint. Tap off any excess paint, and gently press all over the wrapped glove. You want to achieve an aged look. Allow to dry 1 hour.

6 Mix glow-in-the-dark paint with Gloss Mod Podge, using a one-part paint to one-part Mod Podge ratio. Paint a thick coat of the mixture over the entire glove Ⓒ. Allow to dry.

DESIGNER NOTE → *Apply more coats for an even deeper glow.*

7 Turn the glass bowl upside down. Balance it on an object so its lip is off the work surface. Coat the entire outside of the bowl with Gloss Mod Podge.

GLOWING MUMMY HAND CANDY BOWL

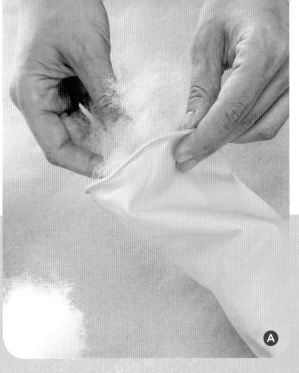

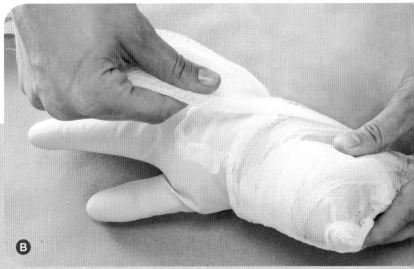

A

B

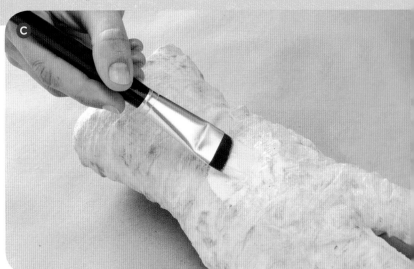

C

8 Position the tissue paper over the bowl Ⓓ. Use your fingers to press the paper down onto the sides of the bowl. Allow the paper to naturally fold and crinkle. Let dry, then apply a topcoat of Mod Podge. Trim the excess paper from the lip of the bowl.

9 Cut skull motifs from the scrapbook paper or fabric. Coat the backs of the motifs with Mod Podge, and position them on the outside of the bowl. Smooth with your fingers. Allow to dry.

10 Hot glue the lace trim and velvet ribbon around the lip of the bowl. Place the mummy hand in the bowl, and fill with candy. Turn the lights off and your mummy hand will cast a spooky glow.

D

BOOK PAGE PUMPKIN WITH MASK

DESIGNER: **Cathie Filian**

I believe that putting a mask on any sort of inanimate object makes that item immediately funny. My goal for this Halloween season is to put a mask on everything, just like Cathie did with this pumpkin. The interest generated by the use of book pages and glitter makes the project worthy to stand alone, but it would also be great in a mantle display grouped with other seasonal décor.

WHAT YOU'LL NEED MOD PODGE TOOL KIT (PAGE 13) ■ GLOSS MOD PODGE ■ PAGES FROM AN OLD BOOK ■ PUMPKIN FORM WITH STEM, CAN BE MADE OF PLASTIC, FOAM, OR PAPIER-MÂCHÉ ■ 1 PIECE OF BURLAP, 6 INCHES (15.2 CM) SQUARE ■ HOT GLUE GUN AND GLUE STICKS ■ MASK TEMPLATE (PAGE 125) ■ BLACK ACRYLIC PAINT ■ BLACK RICKRACK, ENOUGH TO GO AROUND THE PUMPKIN ■ 2 UPHOLSTERY NAILS/BRADS ■ CHUNKY LIME GREEN GLITTER

WHAT YOU DO

1 Cut small squares from the book pages. Each square should be approximately 2 inches (5 cm) square.

2 Use a foam brush to apply the Gloss Mod Podge to a small area of the pumpkin form and to the back of a square. Place the square on the pumpkin and smooth with your fingers. Once it's glued down, brush the square with the Mod Podge.

3 Continue applying the squares Ⓐ as you did in step 2 until the entire pumpkin is covered. Overlap the squares where needed. Allow to dry for one hour.

4 Cut the burlap into three leaf shapes. Use the hot glue to attach them in an overlapping fashion to the pumpkin at the base of the stem.

5 Use the mask template to trace the outline of the mask onto the front of the pumpkin Ⓑ.

6 Fill in the mask with the black paint Ⓒ. Apply several coats of paint, allowing each coat to dry before applying the next.

7 Use the black rickrack for the mask strings. Cut in half, and glue one piece to each side of the mask. Push the upholstery nails into the sides of the mask where the rickrack attaches.

8 Coat the stem of the pumpkin with Mod Podge, and then sprinkle the chunky lime green glitter on it until you've covered the entire stem. Allow to dry.

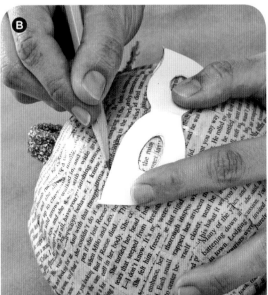

SMILING JACK HALLOWEEN TREAT BOX

DESIGNER: *Julie Lewis*

Vintage jack-o'-lantern faces have been, and will continue to be, popular. I love incorporating them into my Halloween décor and gifts. A treat box like this one can hold candy, be used for trick-or-treating, or even be given as a gift during that spooky time of year. The subtle shimmering effect from the Sparkle Mod Podge gives it that moonlit-night Halloween feel.

WHAT YOU'LL NEED   MOD PODGE TOOL KIT (PAGE 13) ■ SPARKLE MOD PODGE ■ PAPIER-MÂCHÉ BOX ■ ASSORTMENT OF HALLOWEEN-THEMED SCRAPBOOK PAPER ■ 3-INCH (7.6 CM) WOODEN CIRCLE ■ ORANGE SCRAPBOOK PAPER ■ ACRYLIC PAINT IN BLACK, GREEN, ORANGE, AND WHITE ■ HOLOGRAM GLITTER PAINT ■ JACK-O'-LANTERN FACE TEMPLATE (PAGE 125) ■ TRANSFER PAPER AND STYLUS ■ BLACK GLITTERED-SCROLL PAGE EMBELLISHMENTS ■ BLACK POM-POM TRIM (ENOUGH TO GO AROUND THE TOP EDGE OF THE BOX) ■ PIPE CLEANERS IN BLACK-AND-GOLD SPARKLE

WHAT YOU DO

1   Trace the outlines of both the front and back sides of the box on two sheets of the Halloween-themed scrapbook paper. Cut out and set aside.

2   On the back of a piece of orange paper, trace the wooden circle Ⓐ, and set aside.

3   Paint the papier-mâché box with black acrylic paint on the outside and green on the inside. Apply several coats, allowing each coat to dry in between applications.

4   Apply the glitter paint to the inside and outside side panels of the box. Allow to dry.

5   Paint the wood circle with the orange acrylic paint, and allow to dry.

6   Use a medium layer of Mod Podge to glue the cut scrapbook paper to the large front and back sides of the box. Allow to dry for 15 to 20 minutes.

7   Add a medium layer of Mod Podge to glue the orange scrapbook paper (that was set aside in step 2) to the painted wooden circle. Allow to dry for 15 to 20 minutes.

8   Coat both the large sides of the box and the wood circle with Mod Podge, and allow to dry.

9   Transfer the jack-o'-lantern pattern onto the wooden circle using the transfer paper and stylus.

10   Paint the face on the jack-o'-lantern using a fine paintbrush with the black and white acrylic paint Ⓑ. Use the finished project photo as your guide for paint colors or select your own.

11   Glue the jack-o'-lantern face to the center of one of the large sides of the box Ⓒ. Attach the black scroll scrapbook embellishments around the edges as shown.

12   Glue the black pom-pom trim around the top of the box, and then glue the black and gold pipe cleaners to the inside top as handles.

13   Allow to dry for at least 24 hours before carrying or gifting.

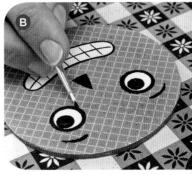

HOLIDAY SEASON GLASS BLOCK

DESIGNER: *Holli Long*

I like all kinds of holiday décor, but I especially like simple and modern. Holli has created a piece that you can use in multiple ways. This glass block looks great on a table during the day, and then, if you're so inclined, you can stick Christmas lights in it for a nighttime glow. You can draw your own motif for your painting pattern, or look for clip art on the web.

WHAT YOU'LL NEED MOD PODGE TOOL KIT (PAGE 13) ◼ FABRIC MOD PODGE ◼ GLOSS MOD PODGE ◼ GLASS BLOCK ◼ HOLIDAY MOTIF TEMPLATE (PAGE 125) ◼ TAPE ◼ ENAMEL GLASS PAINT, IN BLACK, GREEN, AND YELLOW ◼ FABRIC, 1 PIECE LARGE ENOUGH TO FIT ON THE BACK OF THE BLOCK ◼ HOLIDAY LIGHTS (OPTIONAL)

WHAT YOU DO

1 Clean and dry all glass surfaces before painting.

2 If your motif is an outline or tracing, you may want to fill it in to guide you as you paint Ⓐ. Position the pattern with your holiday motif inside the glass block, and tape in place.

3 On the front of the block, use the glass paint with a small brush to paint the motif Ⓑ.

4 Follow the manufacturer's instructions on the glass paint for baking the glass block to cure the paint.

5 Prepare the fabric with Fabric Mod Podge (page 12). Allow to dry. Measure and cut the fabric to fit the back of the glass block. Mod Podge in place, using the Gloss Mod Podge Ⓒ.

6 (Optional) Insert Christmas lights for an added bit of twinkle and shine.

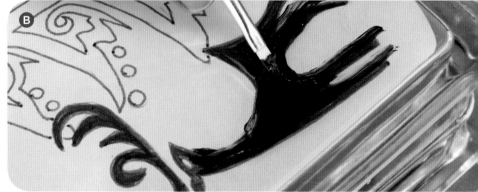

CHEERY RECYCLED GIFT TAGS

With my surplus of oatmeal and cereal boxes, I felt there was something more productive that I could do with them rather than throw them away. I love giving gifts, and I love reusing "stuff"—these gift tags are the perfect combination of those two things. I have a ton of scrap paper and paint on hand so I didn't have to spend any money to make these. That means more to put toward the gift!

WHAT YOU'LL NEED MOD PODGE TOOL KIT (PAGE 13) ■ GLOSS MOD PODGE ■ USED CEREAL BOX
CHRISTMAS SCRAPBOOK PAPER ■ CHRISTMAS EMBELLISHMENTS (WORDS, BRADS, GLITTER, BUTTONS)
RED CHALKBOARD PAINT ■ FOAM BRUSH ■ HOLE PUNCH ■ RIBBON (TO TIE TAG TO GIFT) ■ CHALK

WHAT YOU DO

1 Make a template for cutting out a gift tag. I hand drew mine—you can do it in any shape you like.

2 Using the scissors, cut the tag out of the used cereal box. Use this first tag and the pencil to trace and cut out additional tags.

3 Once all the tags are cut out, trace them onto the back of the scrapbook paper and cut out.

4 Mod Podge the paper to the printed side of the tag Ⓐ. Add a medium coat of Mod Podge, lay down the paper, and smooth thoroughly. Let dry for 15 to 20 minutes.

5 Once dry, paint a topcoat of Mod Podge over the paper Ⓑ, adding embellishments as desired. Allow to dry.

6 Follow the instructions on the chalkboard paint packaging to prepare the painted side of the gift tag.

7 Using the foam brush, paint the prepared side of the tag with chalkboard paint Ⓒ. Apply three additional coats and allow to dry.

8 Make a hole with the hole punch and string a ribbon through.

9 Write the recipient's name on the tag in chalk.

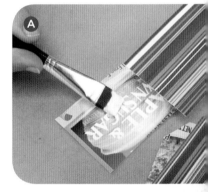

PARTY TIME GIFT BAG

DESIGNER: **Chris Williams**

I'm usually afraid of clowns. To be perfectly honest, they creep me out. But this happy clown on this party bag just puts a huge smile on my face. Thanks to Chris, I'm going to get over my fear and make this project for my next birthday. I figure you're never too old for red-and-white circus stripes or sparkles.

WHAT YOU'LL NEED MOD PODGE TOOL KIT (PAGE 13) ■ MATTE MOD PODGE ■ DIMENSIONAL MAGIC MOD PODGE ■ SPARKLE MOD PODGE ■ RED-AND-WHITE-STRIPED PAPER GIFT BAG ■ CLOWN TEMPLATE (PAGE 124) ■ WHITE PAPER ■ ASSORTMENT OF SCRAPBOOK PAPERS ■ 2 SMALL WHITE STAR BUTTONS ■ YARN SCRAPS ■ HOT GLUE GUN AND GLUE STICKS ■ WOODEN LETTERS TO SPELL PARTY ■ ACRYLIC PAINT IN BLUE AND WHITE ■ TOOTHPICK ■ LARGE POM-POM

WHAT YOU DO

1 Coat the entire bag with a layer of the Matte Mod Podge. Allow to dry.

2 Cut a circle from the white paper for the clown's face, and the elements for the clown's hat and facial features from the assorted scrapbook papers (templates are on page 124).

3 Use Matte Mod Podge to apply the face, hat, and facial features to the bag Ⓐ. Allow to dry for 15 to 20 minutes.

4 Apply two coats of Matte Mod Podge to seal, allowing the first coat to dry before applying the second. Allow to dry.

5 Attach the two small white star buttons to the center of each eye with craft glue.

6 Make loops in the scrap yarn hair by wrapping the yarn four times around three fingers. Secure the loops in the middle with a separate piece of yarn. Make two more of these, and then attach them to the clown's head using hot glue.

7 Cut triangles for the banner from scrapbook paper, and Mod Podge them to the bag.

8 Paint the wooden letters white, and allow to dry. Dip a toothpick in the blue paint, and dot on the letters to create the polka dot pattern. Allow to dry.

9 Apply a coat of Matte Mod Podge over the letters to seal and protect them. Allow to dry, then apply a layer of the Dimensional Magic Mod Podge to the letters to add dimension Ⓑ. Allow to dry.

10 Create small ties from the scrap yarn, and use hot glue to glue them between the banner sections. Glue the letters to the banner using either craft glue or hot glue. Glue the large pom-pom to the clown's hat.

11 Apply a coat or two of the Sparkle Mod Podge to the clown's face and hat Ⓒ. Allow to dry.

PATCHWORK CHRISTMAS ORNAMENTS

DESIGNER: **Julie Lewis**

Some of my most treasured Christmas ornaments are handmade, including the painted pasta from my childhood. Each year I try to add a new handmade ornament. The only requirement is that it is fun enough for my tree—and these patchwork glittery ones by Julie certainly qualify. By the way, does anyone know where I can find that blue tinsel tree I've been looking for?

WHAT YOU'LL NEED MOD PODGE TOOL KIT (PAGE 13) ▪ SPARKLE MOD PODGE ▪ DIMENSIONAL MAGIC MOD PODGE ▪ PAPIER-MÂCHÉ OR WOODEN ORNAMENT BLANKS, ONE FLAT, ONE SIX-SIDED ▪ ASSORTMENT OF WINTER- OR CHRISTMAS-THEMED SCRAPBOOK PAPER ▪ SCRAP PAPER FOR TEMPLATE ▪ SOLID SILVER-COLORED SCRAPBOOK PAPER ▪ 1-INCH (2.5 CM) CIRCLE PUNCH ▪ ACRYLIC PAINT IN METALLIC LIGHT BLUE AND METALLIC SILVER ▪ SMALL ADHESIVE GEMSTWO, ½-INCH (1.3 CM) CLEAR RHINESTONES ▪ 6 METALLIC SILVER PIPE CLEANERS ▪ HOT GLUE GUN WITH GLUE STICKS ▪ CRYSTAL-BEAD DANGLE

WHAT YOU DO

1 Lay the flat papier-mâché or wooden ornament blank on the back of a sheet of scrapbook paper, and trace twice. Cut both shapes out, and then trim off the very top (where the ornament would normally have the hanging cap), and set aside.

2 For the six-sided ornament, make a template of one of the sides using the scrap paper. Use the template to trace six shapes on the assortment of scrapbook paper. Cut out, and set aside.

3 Use the 1-inch (2.5 cm) circle punch to punch six circles from the silver scrapbook paper. Set aside.

4 Paint both ornaments with metallic light blue acrylic paint, and allow to dry. Paint the top of the flat ornament (its hanging cap) with metallic silver. Allow to dry.

5 Use the Sparkle Mod Podge to glue the paper to the ornaments Ⓐ. On the flat ornament, work one side at a time, and allow to dry for 15 to 20 minutes. For the six-sided ornament, work around the ornament, Mod Podging one piece at a time. Allow to dry for 15 to 20 minutes.

6 Apply a coat of Sparkle Mod Podge to each ornament Ⓑ. For the six-sided ornament, Mod Podge a silver circle to the middle of each side. Allow the ornaments to dry before applying a second coat. Allow to dry.

PATCHWORK CHRISTMAS ORNAMENTS

7 On the flat ornament, apply the Dimensional Magic Mod Podge to areas of the designs to make them stand out C. Use craft glue to adhere the small adhesive gems right below the top.

8 On the six-sided ornament, use craft glue to adhere a clear rhinestone in the middle of each silver circle on each side. Trim the pipe cleaners, and use the hot glue to glue them to the seam between each side D.

9 To finish, glue the crystal dangle to the bottom of the six-sided ornament. Allow the ornaments to dry for at least 24 hours before hanging on your tree.

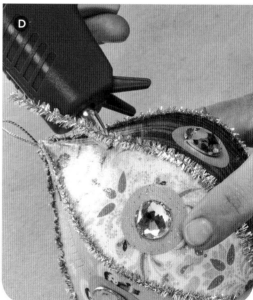

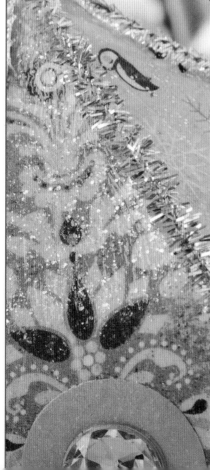

GALLERY

One of the best parts of being a craft blogger is that there's a huge community of us showing off our projects online—so there is no end to the inspiration! I hope you will enjoy this collection of awesome ideas from some of my favorite blogging friends.

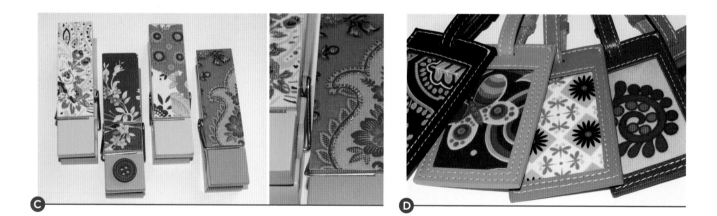

A **Sibylle Roessler**
Denim Shoes
fun.kyti.me
PHOTOS BY ARTIST

B **Melissa Lyn Peda**
Spool Garland
100billionstars.blogspot.com
PHOTOS BY ARTIST

C **Melissa Lyn Peda**
Fridge Magnets
PHOTOS BY ARTIST

D **Melissa Lyn Peda**
Luggage Tags
PHOTO BY ARTIST

E **Stephanie Miller Corfee**
Cash Register
stephaniecorfee.com
PHOTOS BY ARTIST

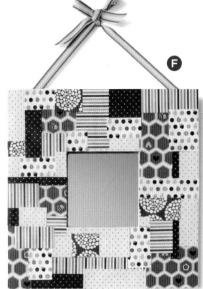

F **Erin Page Bassett**
Paper Quilted Mirror
erinbassett.com
PHOTO BY ARTIST

G **Genevieve Gail Swinford**
Bird's Nest Boxes
genevievegail.com
PHOTO BY ARTIST

H **Stephanie Miller Corfee**
Glasses Case
stephaniecorfee.com
PHOTO BY ARTIST

I **Jennifer Nicole McAliley**
Cute Summer Clutch
scissorsandspatulas.com
PHOTO BY ARTIST

E **Cindy L. Hopper**
Pumpkin and
Ghost Luminaries
skiptomylou.org
PHOTO BY ARTIST

F **Jessica Starr Mundt**
Dresser Drawer Knobs
starr-design.cr.com
PHOTO BY ARTIST

G **Nicole Maki**
Stools
madebynicole.blogspot.com
PHOTOS BY ARTIST

H **Cathie Filian**
Frankenstein
cathieandsteve.com
PHOTO BY ARTIST

I **Jessica Starr Mundt**
Framed Artwork
starr-design.cr.com
PHOTOS BY ARTIST

PARTY TIME GIFT BAG

PAGE 114

**PUMPKIN WITH MASK, HALLOWEEN TREAT BOX,
HOLIDAY SEASON GLASS BLOCK**

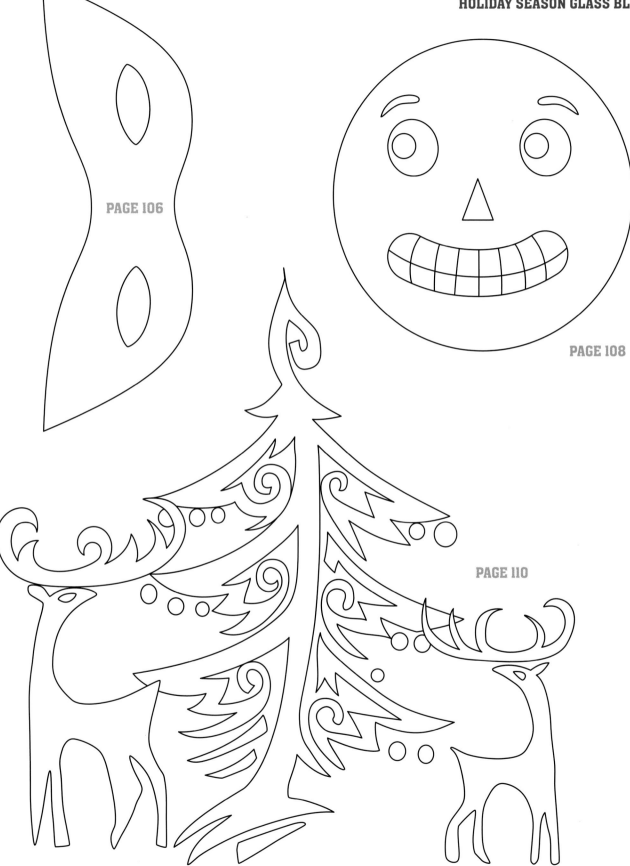

PAGE 106

PAGE 108

PAGE 110

CONTRIBUTING DESIGNERS

Candie Cooper is a jewelry designer with a passion for combining unique materials and color combinations, inspired by her years of living in China. Currently she's creating designs for a variety of companies in the craft industry as well as for craft and jewelry-making publications. Candie is the author of *Metalworking 101 for Beaders* (Lark Crafts 2009) and *Felted Jewelry* (Lark Crafts 2007). You can see more of her work at www.candiecooper.com.

Jenny Doh is founder of www.crescendoh.com, a site that features fresh and creative content from artists and crafters, coupled with stories that highlight the power of art in people's lives. She is author of *Signature Styles*, *Hand in Hand*, *We Make Dolls!*, and co-author of *Where Women Create Book of Inspiration* (all published by Lark Crafts). Jenny lives with her husband and their two children in Santa Ana, California.

Beckie Farrant is a Midwest mom of two who lives for the next project. She repurposes, paints, sews, decoupages, and redesigns anything she can get her hands on. She is a think-outside-the-box crafter who isn't afraid to take chances when it comes to new ideas. Beckie teaches and inspires readers on her blog Infarrantly Creative (infarrantlycreative.net), where she chronicles her creative journey.

Cathie Filian created, produces, and co-hosts the popular lifestyle show, *Creative Juice* on DIY Network & HGTV. In 2007, she was nominated for an Emmy in the Outstanding Lifestyle host category for her work on *Creative Juice*. Cathie has also produced and co-hosted the mini series *Witch Crafts* (on DIY network), which was nominated for two Emmys in 2008. Cathie is the author of *101 Tees*, *101 Snappy Fashions*, and *Bow Wow WOW* (all published by Lark Crafts). Visit her at www.cathieandsteve.com.

Jen Hadfield is a mom of four and the woman behind the DIY craft/decorating blog, Tatertots & Jello. She loves sharing creative tutorials and inspiration every day and you can usually find her knee-deep in her latest project at tatertotsandjello.com.

Julie Lewis graduated from the Cleveland Institute of Art in 1979 with a B.F.A. in Graphic Design. Since then she has worked as a designer in several industries in Ohio including industrial advertising, corporate design, and as a creator for American Greetings. She now resides in Georgia and has spent the last 18 years working as a designer for the largest craft company, Plaid Enterprises, as well as a freelance designer. Julie also has success with her Etsy shop, Stellalola, selling original paintings and felt soft sculptures.

Holli Long started making hundreds of store models and sales samples 20 years ago for Plaid Enterprises. She's used every product that Plaid distributes, making unique projects for them to showcase in books, magazines, trade shows, packaging, and online. Holli loves to decorate her California beach condo and always has a project in the works. She especially enjoys decoupaging and stenciling.

Heather Mann of Dollar Store Crafts specializes in transforming inexpensive materials into stylish and simple craft projects. She shares a cool craft idea every day at DollarStoreCrafts.com.

Chris Myer Williams has always found comfort and happiness when she was busy designing and creating. She has many interests and talents but while decorative painting is her first love, a close second is decoupaging with Mod Podge. Working in the craft and hobby industry for many years, she has enjoyed traveling, teaching, and sharing with others basic crafting how-to's. Chris is the Marketing Education Director and Design Studio Manager at Plaid Enterprises.

MOD PODGE® ROCKS!

ABOUT THE AUTHOR

Amy Anderson, creator of Mod Podge Rocks (www.modpodgerocks-blog.com), is a 30-something transplant from Seattle living in Atlanta, Georgia. She was born from creative genes and is carrying on the tradition through blogging. Amy has been knitting for 19 years, sewing for longer, and decoupaging for just a few. She does all of these things on a daily basis, or at least as much as she can. In addition to Mod Podge, Amy loves the color blue, dogs, reading, cold weather, funny movies, road rallies, yogurt, garden gnomes, sock monkeys, running, tattoos, being outdoors, buttons, snuggling, and apparently blogging.

ACKNOWLEDGMENTS

Thanks to my mother for making me take art classes and go to sewing camp, even when I didn't want to. I wouldn't be creative without you! The designers in this book are owed a big thank you—I love you all. Steve, you are an amazing photographer; don't ever forget it. To my Mod Podge Rocks readers, there aren't enough words to thank you for supporting me these last several years. You rock!

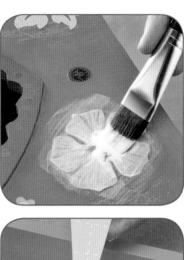

INDEX